☆☆ CONTENTS ☆☆

The crowd waits impatiently. People mill about, restless. They talk to one another in hushed voices. The amphitheater is completely packed, standing room only, but no one minds. They're all just happy to be there and eager to see the show.

The opening act, Kellie Pickler, has already come and gone. Now the stage is dark. Finally, a lone figure emerges from backstage and walks out. The only lights on stage are dimly lit—not enough for the crowd to clearly see the young woman who is heading toward center stage. A spotlight finally kicks on, flooding the whole stage with light and revealing a tall, slender young woman. She steps confidently up to the microphone, her long, wavy, blond hair streaming around her, a silver minidress catching the light and reflecting it back to the crowd. Tall, brown cowboy boots complete the ensemble.

She has a guitar slung comfortably around her neck, and she smiles out at everyone.

"The best first date ever," she announces, starting to strum her guitar, "has nothing to do with where you go to dinner." The crowd is already starting to cheer and sway with the few tune-up chords that come from the young woman's guitar. "The best first date ever has nothing to do with if somebody brings you flowers." An enormous screen hung across the back wall shows the young performer's face larger than life as she continues to speak and strum her guitar. The rest of her band takes their places on the main stage. Her blue eyes look out at the crowd, flashing with excitement, daring the audience to feel the same thrill she does, to listen to the rhythm and the words and let the music carry them away.

"The best first date happens," she finally declares, "when you're with a person who makes you feel fearless!"

Screams and cheers and whistles erupt throughout the amphitheater, and the singer's smile grows wider. Backing away from the microphone for a moment, she strums a bit more and turns to greet the audience members sitting to the side of the stage before returning and starting to sing.

Taylor Swift's Fearless concert tour has just begun. And the young lady in question, clearly fearless herself, is obviously enjoying every minute of it.

And why shouldn't she? It's not every nineteen-year-old who gets to headline her own national concert tour! But Taylor Swift is hardly your average girl. At least not as far as what she's already accomplished. The tour—which promotes her second album, *Fearless*—is just the newest achievement for this incredibly talented, but surprisingly modest and down-to-earth, country singer. She's worked hard to get to this spot, spending years writing songs and performing as the opening act for other bands. Now it's her turn in the spotlight. And Taylor Swift is clearly having a blast.

CHAPTER 1

Little Girl with Big Dreams

Long before she took the stage at the opening night of her Fearless tour, Taylor was just a regular girl growing up in Pennsylvania.

When Taylor's parents, Scott and Andrea Swift, got married, they moved to a small Christmas tree farm in Wyomissing, Pennsylvania, just outside of Reading. The newlyweds were ambitious and practical. Scott was a financial advisor for Merrill Lynch. "Business-wise, he's brilliant," Taylor proudly told the *Ottawa Citizen* about her father. In addition to being a supportive wife, Andrea was also a no-nonsense career woman focused on climbing the corporate ladder. "Before [my mom] had me, she was this really big business executive that worked for an ad agency. I really look up to that. I respect that she had a career on her own and lived alone. She had me when she was 30. She had a complete career of her own and was supporting herself," Taylor told GACtv.com. Together, the two were very happy, but they wanted to start a family. So they were overjoyed when Andrea discovered she was pregnant with their first child in early 1989.

On December 13, 1989, the proud new parents welcomed a baby girl into the world. Andrea was ecstatic about the arrival of her daughter, and she had a very strong opinion about what her new baby's name should be. "She named me Taylor so that if anybody saw on a business card the name, Taylor, they wouldn't know if it was a girl or a guy if they were thinking of hiring me," Taylor explained to the *Toronto Star*. Andrea wanted to make sure that her daughter had every advantage should she decide to take on the business world; she just never thought it would be the music business that Taylor would conquer.

After Taylor was born, Andrea became a full-time mom—well, for most of the year, anyway. Every December, Andrea would spearhead the Swift family's side business—selling Christmas trees from their farm. But she always saved the best tree for her own home! Taylor has always been glad that her mother was home when she was little. "My mom decided to stay home to raise me. She totally raised me to be logical and practical. I was brought up with such a strong woman in my life and I think that had a lot to do with me not wanting to do anything halfway," Taylor told the *Ottawa Citizen*. Andrea lavished her daughter with encouragement, making sure that baby Taylor flourished.

And flourish she did! "I was raised on a little farm and for me when I was little, it was the biggest place in the world. And it was the most magical, wonderful place in the world," Taylor explained to the *Ottawa Citizen*. Even from an early age, Taylor was determined. She was quick to decide what she wanted and go after it. All of the holiday visitors who came to buy trees from the Swift's farm were completely charmed by Taylor. And the visitors fascinated Taylor, too. Her mother told GACtv.com, "From day one, Taylor was always trying to figure out how other people thought and what they were doing and why they were doing it. That was probably an early telltale sign that she had the makings of a songwriter."

When Taylor was two, her mother announced that she was expecting again—Taylor was going to be a big sister! Taylor was probably pretty excited when her brother, Austin, was born. As the two siblings grew, they bonded quickly and loved playing games, watching cartoons, and goofing off together.

The Swifts loved life on the farm, but some of their favorite times as a family were their vacations to the beach in Stone Harbor, New Jersey. As Taylor explained to searay.com, "At the age of four, I lived in a lifejacket. We've always been able to establish and maintain a family atmosphere even when we're far from home, and I think all those years going to the shore helped that."

Taylor and Austin soon grew into tall, energetic kids. They went to the Wyncroft School in Pottstown, Pennsylvania, for elementary school. Taylor excelled at English and creative writing. She even won a national poetry contest when she was in fourth grade. Austin was a natural athlete, but despite a height advantage, Taylor was not. "Everybody thought I'd be good at basketball, but then I tried out and it was, like 'Oh.' I was awful at anything that's sports,"

Taylor explained to the *Ottawa Citizen*.

Luckily, Taylor was a natural at something else—performing. From a very early age, she loved to ham it up. By the time Taylor was two, she was already entertaining her family, their friends, and even strangers with her singing. Her favorite songs to perform were tunes from Disney movies, as she told the *Philadelphia Inquirer*. "There are videos of me walking up to strangers and singing songs from *The Lion King* when I was a baby." Not that this was always a good thing! "I was like four and would run up to people on the beach, like random strangers and just start singing for them," Taylor admitted to *Teen Vogue*, "and [my family] would never know where I was, they were always running after me trying to figure out who I was harassing at the moment." Fortunately, the Swifts just had to follow Taylor's voice!

Andrea and Scott probably weren't too surprised that they had a little songbird on their hands. Andrea's mother had been a professional opera singer and Taylor seemed to have inherited her grandmother's gift for performing. "My grandparents lived all over the world," Taylor told *Wood&Steel*. "In Puerto Rico, my grandmother was the hostess of the top-rated TV variety show, called *The Pan-American Show*. Nanny's Spanish was so bad that the Puerto Ricans thought she was hysterically funny! She went on to become the 'Madrina' [symbolic grandmother figure] of their Air Force; they really loved her. She starred in a lot of operas and was a member of the Houston Grand Opera. I think that's where I got most of my musical ability." Taylor and her grandmother were very close and she was one of Taylor's biggest musical mentors. Having a performer in the family probably helped Taylor's parents prepare for the future they didn't yet realize was in store for them. "My mom was always stuck sitting backstage somewhere or sitting in a front row, watching a performance her entire childhood," Taylor explained to *Rolling Stone*. "She thought when her mom stopped performing she was relieved of those duties, but all I wanted to do was sing, ever since I was born, so she's always been backstage."

Taylor's grandmother wasn't the only musical influence in her life. When she was six, Taylor received her first LeAnn Rimes album, *Blue,* and discovered country music. "I just really loved how she could be making music and having a career at such a young age," she admitted to *Rolling Stone.* Talk about a role model! LeAnn was one of the biggest teen country stars of all time, releasing her first album when she was only thirteen years old and making it into the record books as the first country artist ever to receive the Grammy's Best New Artist award. So it's no surprise that little Taylor wanted to follow in her footsteps.

Taylor listened to that album nonstop and, soon, she could perform all of LeAnn's songs. "I knew every song she ever sang. After that, I kind of went back and learned the history. I listened to legends like Dolly [Parton] and Patsy Cline—women who were the essence of country music," Taylor told GACtv.com. It didn't take long before Taylor was hooked on country music. "I was influenced early on by all of the great female country artists of the '90s and all of the cool music they were putting out. Like Shania [Twain], Faith [Hill], the Dixie Chicks. It was such great music, and it completely drew me in to country music," Taylor explained to CMT.com.

That particular trio of female performers appealed to Taylor for other reasons as well, though. "I think the thing that cemented it in my mind and made me fall in love with country music was seeing three great examples of what females could bring to country music," she told *Rolling Stone*. "I saw that Shania Twain brought this independence and this crossover appeal; I saw that Faith Hill brought this classic old-school glamour and beauty and grace; and I saw that the Dixie Chicks brought this complete 'we don't care what you think' quirkiness, and I loved what all of those women were able to do and what they were able to bring to country music."

Taylor couldn't stop singing along to her country albums, so her mom encouraged her to try out for the children's community theater when she was nine. Taylor took to the stage immediately. She had a blast acting, but she loved performing in musicals the best. It was onstage at the theater that Taylor finally realized that being a country music singer was what she wanted to do for the rest of her life. "I was playing the role of Sandy in *Grease* and it just came out sounding country. It was all I had listened to so I guess it was just kind of natural. I decided country music was what I needed to be doing," Taylor told GACtv.com. Taylor wasn't the only one who noticed a decidedly country twang to her vocals. As Andrea explained to searay.com, everyone else who saw Taylor's performance realized it, too. When Taylor took the stage to belt out her big solo, "Hopelessly Devoted To You," another parent leaned in to Andrea and Scott and whispered, "You have a great little country singer there."

Once Taylor had performed in front of an audience, there was no going back. She loved being onstage under the bright lights, basking in the rounds of applause, and, most of all, expressing herself through music. Taylor had always loved singing, but when she performed in front of a live audience, she felt complete. She knew then that she wanted to be a professional singer. And not just any professional singer. Taylor wanted to be the next big country music star.

CHAPTER 2

Developing Talent

Once Taylor made up her mind to become the next country star, she got right to work chasing her big dream. Taylor already knew all of the words to her favorite country songs, so she started with karaoke performances. There were a few bars and restaurants in the area that hosted karaoke nights, and Taylor made sure she performed in every one of them that she could. She really had to beg her parents to take her when the karaoke nights were in bars, which weren't necessarily the most appropriate places for a ten-year-old girl to be hanging out. "[My mom and dad] were kind of embarrassed by it, I guess. This little girl singing in this smoky bar. But they knew how much it meant to me so they went along with it," Taylor explained to GACtv.com.

Eventually, Scott and Andrea were won over by their daughter's enthusiasm and dedication and began helping her line up gigs, even in bars. "I think people should never ever put an age limit on what someone can accomplish," Taylor told GACtv.com. "My parents, ever since the day I was born, have empowered me. There are really two ways to look at it when you are raising kids. You can either say 'You can be whatever you want to be' and then there is actually believing it. My parents actually believed it."

One of Taylor's favorite karaoke spots was the Pat Garrett Roadhouse in Strausstown, Pennsylvania, halfway between Allentown and Harrisburg. Pat Garrett is a country singer who had a few hits in the early 1980s and then settled down in Pennsylvania. In addition to his Roadhouse, Pat also owns and runs the Pat Garrett Amphitheater, where tons of country acts come to perform. Pat would sponsor karaoke nights a few times a week and would offer the winner a chance to open for whichever country act was performing at his amphitheater. "I started out singing karaoke in [Pat Garrett's] roadhouse—his little bar—when I was 10 years old. He'll vouch that I was there every single week saying, 'I'm just going to come back if you don't let me win one.' I was kind of like an annoying fly around that place. I just would not leave them alone. What they would do is have these karaoke contests. And if you won, you got to open for, like, Charlie Daniels or George Jones. I would go until I would win," Taylor explained to CMT.com.

As a result of her determination and talent, Taylor got the chance to open for Charlie Daniels and several other country acts when she was only ten years old! She was nervous at first, especially since she was usually the only child performing! As she recounted to CMT.com, "I started singing in front of crowds when I was 10, and it was a little scary at first. Anything you've just started doing is going to be scary. Once, somebody told me to picture the audience in their underpants. Do *not* picture the audience in their underpants. That does not work. At all." It turned out that her love of performing was all Taylor really needed to get over her nervousness, and she nailed her opening act performances.

Taylor's standout karaoke act quickly earned her a reputation in the area, and she was soon performing at fairs and festivals throughout the state. Taylor jumped at every opportunity to perform and earn new fans, and impressed fair promoters and organizers with her professionalism and drive. "Every single weekend, I would go to festivals and fairs and karaoke contests—any place I could get up on stage. The cool thing about this is that my parents have never pushed me. It's always been [my] desire and love to do this. That's what makes this so sweet. If I had been pushed, if I didn't love this, I would probably not have been able to get this far," Taylor told CMT.com. Andrea and Scott were happy as long as Taylor was happy, and nothing made Taylor happier than singing in front of a crowd. So, while all of the other girls her age were having sleepovers, playing in pools, and hanging at the mall, Taylor was singing her heart out every weekend.

In addition to fairs and festivals, Taylor also sang the national anthem at a number of sporting events. One of her highest-profile gigs was performing at the start of a Philadelphia 76ers game, when a musical heavyweight just happened to be in the audience. "When I was 11, I sang the national anthem at a

76ers game in Philly. Jay-Z was sitting courtside and gave me a high five after I sang. I bragged about that for like a year straight," Taylor reminisced to CMT.com. Taylor has a lot of respect for the rap and hip-hop mogul and it was a huge compliment to have him recognize her ability—even if it was just a high five. It was certainly a sign that Taylor was more talented than the average eleven-year-old!

Riding high on successes like these, Taylor had her mother help her record a demo CD when she was eleven. It contained several tracks of Taylor singing karaoke to classic country songs. Taylor knew that if she wanted a record deal, she was going to have to get the attention of the bigwigs of country music in Nashville, Tennessee. Nashville has long been the center of the country music world, which is why it's known as Music City. It's the home of the famed Ryman Auditorium, the Grand Ole Opry, and Tootsie's Orchid Lounge. All of Taylor's favorite country artists had gotten their big breaks on Nashville's Music Row, a well-known street where most country music labels' offices are located. Since Taylor had her heart set on following in the boot prints of Patsy Cline, Faith Hill, LeAnn Rimes, and the Dixie Chicks, she and her mother made copies of her demo CD and drove down to Nashville. It took a lot of courage to put herself out there like that, especially knowing that most people who want to be stars never make it. But Taylor didn't let the thought of failure stop her. She believed in herself so much that she thought she would come home with a record deal for sure. As Taylor explained to GACtv.com, "I was like, if I want to sing music, I'm going to need a record deal. So, I'm going to get a record deal. I thought it was that easy. I made a demo tape of me singing along to karaoke songs and my mom and I started walking up and down Music Row handing them out to receptionists at every label. I think I had one person call me back. And he was so sweet, just kind of telling me, 'You know, this is not how you do this.'"

Taylor didn't get a recording contract on that trip to Nashville, but she did learn some valuable lessons. She went home to Wyomissing more determined than ever to break into country music. She learned that she needed to find a way to make herself stand out from the hundreds of other wannabe stars. After all, Taylor was young, beautiful, and had amazing singing and performing skills, but that wasn't enough when everyone she was competing with could claim the same thing. She just had to figure out what made her unique and try again.

All in all, things were going well for Taylor. She was performing as often as possible, and even though her first trip to Nashville hadn't gone exactly as planned, she had a much better idea of what she needed to work on to eventually score a record deal. So Taylor was pretty happy with life when she started seventh grade at Wyomissing Junior High School. She must have been excited to move to a bigger school with more opportunities for her to study music and tons of new classmates to perform for!

Unfortunately, Taylor was disappointed with her new school. It seemed that her dedication to her craft and her musical success had alienated her from her classmates, and she suddenly found that her friends from elementary school wanted nothing more to do with her. "It was a really lonely time in my life," Taylor explained to the *Philadelphia Inquirer*. "I was friends with a group of girls, and then I wasn't friends with them anymore, and I didn't know why." Taylor was very hurt by the rejection of her peers and she couldn't figure out what she needed to say or do to get back in with the other kids. "I was not included. I would go to school some days, a lot of days, and not know who I was going to talk to. And that's a really terrifying thing for somebody who's 12," Taylor confessed to the *Toronto Star*.

Despite her troubles at school, Taylor tried to keep her spirits up. "I'm not quite sure how it affected me to lose all my friends and have to walk into school and go at it alone," she admitted to *CosmoGirl!*, "but I can only hope that it made me a stronger person." Since she didn't have any close friends to hang out with all the time, Taylor threw herself into her music. Then one day when she was twelve, Taylor's computer, which she used to burn CDs of her demo, started acting up. So she called a repairman who turned out to be much more than a computer geek. "I learned to play guitar when this guy came over to fix my computer. He saw that I had [an acoustic guitar] in the corner, and he goes,

'Do you know how to play that? You want me to teach you some chords?' I was like, 'Yeah, sure!' So he taught me three chords," Taylor told GACtv.com. They were G, D, and C, three of the most commonly used chords in music. Taylor played those chords over and over until she had the feel of them. When she strummed that guitar, it was as if everything clicked into place. After the computer repairman left, Taylor sat down with her guitar in hand and wrote her first song using only those three chords. It was called "Lucky You." "The song was about a girl who didn't fit in and she didn't care and she was different than everyone else," Taylor recounted to *Rolling Stone*. Sound familiar?

Songwriting came naturally to Taylor, and she soon found that writing was the perfect way to express herself. She could pour out her emotions, events of the day, and her dreams into the music and lyrics and feel better, no matter how badly she had been feeling before. Performing her own songs was a completely different experience for Taylor. She felt like she was connecting with her audience on a new level, and she soon realized that the fact that she wrote and performed her own music was what could set her apart from other artists.

Freshly motivated by her newfound talent, Taylor set to work practicing guitar every chance she could get. She would rush home from school every day, race through her homework, and then practice as long as she could. "When I picked up the guitar, I could not stop," she told *Rolling Stone*. "I would literally play until my fingers bled—my mom had to tape them up, and you can imagine how popular that made me: 'Look at her fingers, so weird.'" That didn't exactly help Taylor's popularity at school! "But for the first time," she explained, "I could sit in class and those girls could say anything they wanted about me, because after school I was going to go home and write a song about it."

As Taylor's guitar skills grew, so did her collection of original songs. One of the first songs she ever wrote was inspired by seeing LeAnn Rimes in concert and is called "Kid in the Crowd." Another of Taylor's early compositions is called "The Outside," and was one of several songs she wrote about feeling alienated from her classmates at school. "I found myself watching their reactions and their emotions mostly to figure out what I was doing so wrong. But then I realized if I could watch these people and write it all down, it would make a good song," Taylor explained to GACtv.com.

Eighth grade hadn't been any better socially for Taylor than seventh had been. She was still alone most of the time and very few of the girls at school were even friendly to her. A lot of kids would have turned to destructive habits like drugs or alcohol to deal with those feelings of rejection and loneliness, but that was never an option for Taylor, no matter how bad things got. As she explained to the *Toronto Star*, "The thing that I found to escape from any pain . . . was writing songs."

Taylor's parents worried about their suddenly introverted daughter, and hearing the pain in her lyrics nearly broke their hearts. "When she started writing music, some of the first things she wrote about [were] being unhappy and left out. But it was an outlet, so I was thrilled that she found a way to express it and let it go," Andrea told GACtv.com. But Taylor wouldn't trade those two difficult years for anything in the world, because it was going through that rejection that helped her find her voice in songwriting. As she explained to CMT.com, "I found that I was alone a lot of the time, kind of on the outside looking into [my classmates'] discussions, and the things they were saying to each other. They really didn't talk to me . . . I started developing this really keen sense of observation—of how to watch people and see what they did. From that sense, I was able to write songs about relationships when I was 13 but not in relationships."

Through it all, Taylor continued to perform at festivals and fairs, singing her own songs and playing her acoustic guitar. But she still sometimes sang an old classic, the national anthem, and that's the song that gave her one of her biggest breaks. Taylor was asked to belt out America's official song at the U.S. Open tennis tournament when she was thirteen. She was blown away by the honor and gave it all she had. As always, the audience took notice. "While I was singing the National Anthem, the entertainment director for the U.S. Open started asking my dad about me. Afterward, my dad put together this typical 'dad video' type of thing—with the cat chewing the neck of my [guitar], and stuff like that—and sent it to her, not knowing that she was going to send it to [music manager] Dan Dymtrow. Dan called and asked us to come down and play for him in his office, so I brought my first 12-string down and played some songs for them. Dan said, 'I want to work with you guys,' and it's been great ever since! I love Dan—he is an *awesome* manager," Taylor told *Wood&Steel*. At the time Dan Dymtrow was also the manager of pop superstar Britney Spears.

Dan got right to work promoting Taylor, and one of his first acts as her manager was to get her featured in the popular clothing store Abercrombie & Fitch's "Rising Star" campaign. That was a very proud moment for Taylor, who was already a huge fan of Abercrombie's cute distressed jeans, button-downs, and T-shirts. The trendy clothes were a big hit with the girls at Wyomissing Junior High, and Taylor probably felt a certain satisfaction when the girls who had snubbed her so badly saw Taylor highlighted in Abercrombie's advertising campaign!

The Abercrombie campaign was just the

beginning of Dymtrow's plans for Taylor's career. After that, Taylor recorded a new demo album featuring the best of her original songs, and Dymtrow made sure that all of the country music heavy hitters heard it. He shopped the demo around and, as a professional, he was able to get much more attention than Taylor could on her own. The Nashville music labels were intrigued by the young singer and songwriter, and were interested to hear her perform live. When Taylor headed back down to Nashville, she was surrounded by plenty of buzz. This time, Music Row took notice.

After several meetings with different labels, RCA, which stands for Radio Corporation of America, offered thirteen-year-old Taylor a development deal. A development deal meant that RCA was willing to give Taylor money, resources, and studio time to record songs, with no guarantee that they would put out an album. It wasn't quite a record deal, but it was an amazing opportunity for Taylor. The only problem was that RCA was located in Nashville, and Taylor and her family lived in Wyomissing, Pennsylvania. Taylor and her mother took a few trips to Nashville to meet with RCA's songwriters and producers, but it became increasingly difficult to take advantage of RCA's resources from so far away. So, after some soul-searching, Taylor and her family decided to make the move to Nashville so that Taylor could really pursue her career. The Swifts were goin' country—for real!

☆ ☆ CHAPTER 3 ☆ ☆
Moving on Out

Taylor was thrilled about her family's big move. She was ready to leave the difficult years of junior high behind her and really get started pursuing her big dreams in the city where country was king—Nashville, Tennessee. She was sad to leave behind her childhood home and all of her fans from her regular appearances at local festivals, fairs, and karaoke hot spots, but she knew it was worth it. Luckily, Taylor's family was supportive enough of her dreams to make the move for her. "Andrea and Taylor had been road-tripping to Nashville a lot for songwriting and recording sessions, and we realized it might make sense to move," Scott Swift told searay.com.

The Swifts wanted to wait until school let out for the summer to make the actual move, but Andrea began house hunting on their regular trips down to Nashville throughout the spring. Andrea knew she had found the perfect place when she toured an adorable house right on Old Hickory Lake in Hendersonville. Hendersonville is a suburb of Nashville. It's close to the big city, but still had the small-town charm the Swifts were looking for. The rest of the family fell in love with the lake—especially Scott, who told searay.com, "When Andrea found a place on Old Hickory Lake, we stopped at the dock on the way up to check out the house. I looked down the cove toward the lake, imagined my Sea Ray [boat] tied up there and said, 'I'll take it.' She said, 'Don't you want to see the house first?'" The Swifts were in good company in their new home. Music legend Roy Orbison had a home on Old Hickory Lake for twenty years; country's "Man in Black" himself, Johnny Cash, and his wife, June Carter Cash, lived on the lake in an eighteen-room mansion until their deaths in 2003; and Richard Sterban of the Oak Ridge Boys lived nearby. Maybe there's something in that Old Hickory Lake water that helps produce hits!

Once they found their dream home, the Swifts

packed up and moved over the summer. Both Taylor and Austin adjusted to life in Tennessee pretty quickly. When school started in the fall, Austin became involved in sports like football and he quickly found a great group of friends. Taylor was also finally having luck at school. Hendersonville High School was a fresh start for the one-time outsider. Despite her single-minded focus on music after school, during the school day, Taylor began to find her balance socially. In her freshman-year English class, Taylor clicked with a girl named Abigail Anderson and they became fast friends. "We became best friends right away . . . we went through just about everything together," Taylor told GACtv.com. The two girls often got in trouble for being silly in class, and they drove Taylor's parents nuts giggling at their inside jokes. "Me and [my] friend, Abigail, always talk with Minnesota accents and everyone thinks we're weird. When I was in ninth grade, (we) didn't talk in any other voice except *Napoleon Dynamite* the entire year," Taylor explained to the *St. Petersburg Times*. It was nice for Taylor to finally have a best friend, especially after all of those friendless years in junior high. Abigail had no musical aspirations of her own, but she was always super supportive and remains one of Taylor's biggest fans. But not all of Taylor's new classmates understood her, as she explained to GACtv.com. "I sang country music. I played guitar. In class I would sit there writing down lyrics. And I don't think they got that, really." But Taylor's classmates were all impressed by her musical abilities, which she showcased in music classes and school assemblies, and they all thought it was pretty cool to have a budding country star in their midst. "Music has always been my game," Taylor explained to searay.com. "It's my after-school activity. Everyone at school knows it's what I do and they're all really supportive."

Some of Taylor's classmates were bigger fans than others, especially the boys at Hendersonville High! Taylor had always felt out of place and awkward in Wyomissing, but she blossomed in Nashville and the local boys took notice. She had always been confident about her music, but changing schools and interacting with different kids had helped Taylor gain confidence in herself, including her looks. And, at 5'11" without shoes, Taylor literally stood out in a crowd. She began showing off her slender build and long legs more by wearing lots of dresses and skirts. She stopped trying to straighten her blond curls and, instead, grew them even longer, adopting the signature hairstyle that her fans have come to love. Taylor began talking and flirting with boys, and soon she was going on dates and having boyfriends.

One of Taylor's boyfriends, Brandon Borello, inspired Taylor to write "Our Song." Taylor and Brandon, a senior, had been struggling to find a song that described their relationship perfectly—but nothing seemed to fit. When Taylor needed a new song to perform at the Hendersonville High talent show, she decided to write one for her and her boyfriend. Taylor's incredibly catchy love song was the hit of the talent show. As she explained to theboot.com, "I wrote this song in my freshman year of high school for my ninth grade talent show. I was sitting there thinking, 'I've gotta write an upbeat song that's gonna relate to everyone.' And at that time, I was dating a guy and we didn't have a song. So I wrote us one, and I played it at the show.

Months later, people would come up to me and say, 'I loved that song that you played.' And then they'd start singing lines of it back to me. They'd only heard it once, so I thought, 'There must be something here!'"

Taylor may have been shining at Hendersonville High School, but things weren't going as well at RCA. Taylor had been working hard to impress the executives at RCA, but they were still hesitant to put their full weight behind the unknown fourteen-year-old by producing a record for her. They weren't impressed with Taylor's original songs, and wanted her to record other people's songs instead, which wasn't what Taylor wanted for herself. She wanted more attention and direction than the label was willing to give her. As she told *Entertainment Weekly*, "I did not want to be on a record label that wanted me to cut other people's stuff. That wasn't where I wanted to be . . . I didn't want to just be another girl singer. I wanted there to be something that set me apart. And I knew that had to be my writing. Also, it was a big, big record label with big superstars, and I felt like I needed my own direction and the kind of attention that a little label will give you. I just did not want it to happen with the method of 'Let's throw this up against the wall and see if it sticks, and if it doesn't, we'll just walk away.' I wanted a record label that needed me, that absolutely was counting on me to succeed." So, after a year of development, Taylor walked away from RCA and began shopping her demos around to the major labels again. She also parted ways with her manager, Dan Dymtrow, eager for a fresh start.

It was a challenging and frustrating time for Taylor—but she handled it with her usual combination of grace, strength, and persistence. "Being able to face the rejections of Nashville is nothing compared to facing the rejections at middle school," Taylor told the *Miami Herald*. Taylor had her work cut out for her, as she explained to *Entertainment Weekly*. "It's not a really popular thing to do in Nashville, to walk away from a major record deal. But that's what I did, because I wanted to find some place that would really put a lot of time and care into this." That only meant that Taylor had to work extra hard to convince Nashville's major labels to take a chance on her. She met with executive after executive, but they were all wary about making an album with an unknown fourteen-year-old, no matter how talented. Other country stars had started very successful careers in their teens, such as LeAnn Rimes, Dolly Parton, and Tanya Tucker, but even more had failed. "I can understand," Taylor told CMT.com. "They were afraid to put out a 13-year-old. They were afraid to put out a 14-year-old. Then they were afraid to put out a 15-year-old. Then they were nervous about putting out a 16-year-old."

Luckily, Taylor didn't give up. She kept pushing for what she wanted, and she was talented enough to get it. Sony/ATV certainly took notice of the pretty fourteen-year-old and her original compositions. They didn't offer Taylor a record deal, but they did offer her a job. They signed Taylor on to a publishing deal as a house writer, the youngest house writer in their history! Taylor was thrilled to have someone recognize her for her songwriting talents and she couldn't wait to get to work.

☆☆ CHAPTER 4 ☆☆
School of Song

Taylor was thrilled to begin her after-school job, but she knew she was going to have to work harder than every other songwriter at Sony. Being a talented fourteen-year-old writer wouldn't be enough—Taylor was determined to be one of the best songwriters of any age, but she was also determined to keep working toward getting her own record out. "I signed my publishing deal at age 14 with Sony/ATV," Taylor explained to songwriteruniverse.com. "I signed and worked with (exec) Arthur Buenahora, who was great. When I signed, I knew that I had to work just as hard as the veteran 45-year-old writers who were also signed there. I wrote a lot of songs, which were mainly for my own artist project, rather than writing songs for pitching to other artists." When Taylor finally got the chance to record her own album, she wanted to make sure she was ready—with enough single-worthy tunes to fill her debut ten times over! Of course, Taylor was allowed to keep any of the songs she wrote for herself, but if it was a song she knew she wouldn't record, other artists could consider it for their albums. With that kind of motivation, her bosses never had to push her. Taylor pushed herself harder than anyone else ever could have.

Taylor used her age and her experiences to her advantage when it came to her songwriting—she wrote what she was feeling as a young teenage girl, hoping that other teenage girls could relate. As she explained to the *Ontario Star*, "I think I've been inspired by things that have actually happened. I can't sit down and write about something I've never felt before. The songs I write in 15 minutes—because they're just so fast, they just come to me—are about things I've gone through." She also told GACtv.com, "Whatever you're feeling that day, it comes out of you. It's kind of like photography—looking at a little picture album of where you are emotionally. I now consider myself a songwriter first and foremost, and I have never written anything I didn't mean."

Of course, not every song Taylor wrote was up to her incredibly high standards. She often spent days editing a song, only to put it away knowing she would never record it. Even if Taylor knew she wouldn't use a song, she still wanted to finish what she had started to the best of her ability.

Taylor's greatest source of inspiration was her high school and the people she knew there. She often wrote about her classmates, and she was never shy about including personal details. Taylor likes calling people out in her music, especially when it comes to boys who break her heart. "When you go through a horrible breakup—from someone you should never have dated in the first place—it's a waste of effort. But if you write a song about the experience it's not a wasted experience, it helped the career," Taylor explained to the *Miami Herald*.

Taylor doesn't let any experience go to waste— she even writes songs about boys she didn't date, or wants to date, or boys who break her friends' hearts. "You listen to my [songs] and it sounds like I've had 500 boyfriends. But that's really not the case. I found that you don't have to date someone to write a song about them," Taylor explained to CMT.com.

Sometimes Taylor found that inspiration hit at the worst possible times—like in the middle of class. "Writing a song . . . you don't feel like you're really doing it. You feel like the song is coming to you, sometimes, and you can't really choose when that happens. I used to be at school and my teachers and classmates would all think I was weird because I would have to get up and go to the bathroom and record a melody into my phone so I could remember it," Taylor told the *St. Petersburg Times*. And boring classes were just more chances to polish her craft, as Taylor told GACtv.com. "If we had random notebook checks, my teachers might find biology notes . . . biology notes . . . then suddenly a bunch of lyrics." Luckily, Taylor was such a good student that it didn't hurt her grades if she spent a little bit of time writing songs during class.

To help their newest employee perfect her songs and hone her songwriting skills, Sony paired Taylor up with one of their veteran songwriters, Liz Rose. In over twenty years in the business, Liz had never met anyone like Taylor, even if she was a little apprehensive at first about taking on such a young partner. "She's probably the finest singer-songwriter I've ever worked with," Liz told the *Associated Press*. "She's a genius, coming in with ideas and a melody. She'd come in and write with this old lady, and I never second-guessed her. I respect her a lot." Liz and Taylor wrote together once a week, and Liz came to look forward to those writing sessions as her easiest of the week. "She always came in with an idea. Most of her songs are about something she has just gone through that day or that weekend. She is so fast and so good. But it's not that she's in a hurry. It's that she's got to get it *out*," Liz told GACtv.com.

Liz was blown away by Taylor's professional attitude. "We wrote every Tuesday at four in the afternoon. She'd blow into the office and you'd hear about her day at school—this is what happened to some girl or some guy. She'd grab a handful of chocolate, walk into the writer's room, and shut the door. Until she got into that room, she was teenager. But once that door closed—she was a writer," Rose told GACtv.com. The two quickly developed a friendship, despite the difference in their ages. "I love writing with Liz," Taylor gushed to songwriteruniverse.com. "When we write, I usually come in with a melody and some lyric content, and then we'll work on creating the rest of the song. She's a really good song editor." Taylor claims she could never have written her hit songs without Liz, but Liz disagrees. "I laugh when people call me a cowriter. I just take dictation," Liz laughingly told GACtv.com.

One of the first songs Liz and Taylor worked on together was a bittersweet love song about Taylor's boyfriend Brandon Borello. Brandon was a senior who was getting ready to leave for college and Taylor knew their relationship was soon going to end. "I wrote [the song] in my freshman year of high school. I got the idea in math class. I was just sitting there, and I started humming this melody. I kind of related it to this situation I was in. I was dating a guy who was about to go off to college. I knew we were going to break up. So I started thinking about all the things that I knew would remind him of me. Surprisingly, the first thing that came to mind was that my favorite country artist is Tim McGraw,"

Taylor told CMT.com. "Tim McGraw" became the name of the tune and Taylor burst into her Tuesday meeting with Liz ready to get it on paper. As Liz told GACtv.com, "With 'Tim McGraw' she came in with the idea and melody. She knew exactly what she wanted." Writing about their impending split really helped ease the pain of saying good-bye for Taylor. Brandon was Taylor's first long-term boyfriend and they meant a lot to each other, but they knew it would be crazy to try to make a long-distance relationship work. "I dated him for about a year and we are still friends . . . He really thought it was cool that, [even though] we weren't going out anymore, I remembered our relationship nicely," Taylor told GACtv.com. That song, and that breakup, would turn out to be one of the best things to ever happen to Taylor. When Taylor did finally get a record deal, "Tim McGraw" would be her first single!

Taylor also wrote her second single, "Teardrops On My Guitar," with Liz's help. At the beginning of her sophomore year, Taylor had a huge crush on one of Hendersonville High's star wrestlers, Drew Hardwick. They were friends, but Drew had no idea how Taylor felt about him, as Taylor explained to *Country Standard Time.* "I used to have a huge crush on this guy, Drew, who would sit there every day talking to me about another girl: how beautiful she was, how nice and smart and perfect she was. I sat there and listened and said, 'Oh, I'm so happy for you.' I guess this is a good example of how I let my feelings out in songs and sometimes no other way. I love this song because of its honesty and vulnerability. To this day, Drew and his girlfriend are still together." Giving Drew advice on how to woo the girl of his dreams was agony for Taylor. She struggled with her crush for most of her sophomore year and was relieved to pour her feelings out into a song. With Liz's help, Taylor managed to capture exactly how she was feeling. After the song was finished, Taylor knew that there were plenty of girls out there who would eventually listen to her song and relate to her situation.

Taylor penned the angry country rock tune "Picture To Burn" about another guy who was never her boyfriend. "We almost dated. It really bothered me that he was so cocky and that's where that song came from. After school, I would write songs every single day, exactly what I felt. I found myself just sitting there with my guitar going, 'I hate his stupid truck that he doesn't let me drive. He's such a redneck! Oh my God!' That actually became the chorus to the song, so that's one of the most honest songs I've ever written," Taylor told GACtv.com. Taylor wrote one final breakup song a week before her last recording session with Liz when she found out that the boy she was dating, Sam, had cheated on her. Taylor isn't the type of girl to let something like that slide, so she immediately ended the relationship and put her anger into the song, "Should've Said No." "Basically, it's about a guy who cheated on me and shouldn't have because I write songs," she told CMT.com. Sam probably regrets cheating on Taylor now!

But not all of Taylor's songs are about romantic love. "There's one [song] on the album called 'Tied Together With a Smile' that I wrote about one of my friends, who is this beauty queen, pageant princess— a gorgeous, popular girl in high school. Every guy wanted to be with her, every girl wanted to be her. I wrote that song the day I found out she had an eating disorder," Taylor told *Entertainment Weekly*. Taylor was devastated that such a beautiful girl could have so little self-confidence. The girl has since gotten help and is doing much better, but Taylor hates that any girl could feel that way. If it was up to her, every girl would feel beautiful and special all of the time, and she hopes that her songs empower her fans. If you or anyone you know is suffering from an eating disorder, there are tons of places to go for help, like the National Eating Disorders Association's website, nationaleatingdisorders.org. Taylor wants her fans to take care of themselves, and that includes asking for help sometimes.

While Taylor was writing for Sony, she was introduced to a demo producer named Nathan Chapman. Nathan and Taylor clicked immediately and the two worked closely together to create demos of the songs Taylor was writing. "I started off with this demo producer who worked in a little shed behind this publishing company I was at. His name was Nathan Chapman. I'd always go in there and play him some new songs, and the next week he would have this awesome track, on which he played every instrument, and it sounded like a record. We did this for a period of a year to two years before I got my record deal," Taylor told CMT.com.

Taylor developed a real rapport with Nathan and it showed in how well her demos came out. Those demos began to catch the attention of record executives on Music Row. Since Sony hadn't offered Taylor a record deal, she continued working for them as a songwriter, but kept taking her demos to different label executives. They were all watching Taylor, waiting to see how her skills would develop as she grew. One executive in particular, Scott Borchetta, was especially interested in Taylor, but he was waiting for the right moment to make his move. Scott invited Taylor to his office at DreamWorks, where he was a Senior Vice President of Promotion and Artist Development. She played him a few of her songs live and he was very impressed with what he heard. "Still to this day, it never hit me that Taylor was a teenager. To me, she was a hit songwriter," Scott told CMT.com. Scott was gearing up to revolutionize the country music scene, and he had a feeling there was a perfect place for Taylor in his vision.

☆☆ CHAPTER 5 ☆☆
Building a Big Machine

Taylor spent the summer after her freshman year of high school gearing up for a very important songwriters showcase at Nashville's famous Bluebird Cafe. The Bluebird Cafe has a well-deserved reputation for launching country stars including Garth Brooks. Everyone who's anyone in the Nashville music scene flocks to the Bluebird for the chance to see the first public performance of a future star or hit songwriter. As the youngest performer that night, Taylor stood out. "It was kind of an intimidating scene," Taylor told the *Denver Westword*. But Taylor was more than ready for that performance, and she proved to everyone in the room why she was there.

One audience member in particular was paying special attention to Taylor's performance. Scott

Borchetta had met with Taylor several weeks before her showcase. He was already impressed with Taylor, but he was blown away by her stage presence and charisma at the Bluebird. "Out of all the people in the room, he was the only one who had his eyes closed and was totally into the music," Taylor told GACtv.com. Taylor never could have guessed the real reason he was there.

Scott wasn't looking to sign Taylor to DreamWorks. He wanted to sign Taylor to a new label, one he was about to create! Scott certainly had the experience to run his own label, having guided the careers of some of Music City's biggest stars including Toby Keith, George Strait, Reba McEntire, Trisha Yearwood, Shania Twain, Sugarland, and Lee Ann Womack. Still, Scott's plan was a huge risk for everyone involved.

A few weeks later, Taylor received a very mysterious phone call from Scott. "He was like, 'I'm going to be doing something and I need to talk to you in person because I don't trust the phone.' And I was like, 'If you don't trust the phone there has got to be something going on that I want to know about.' And when I heard what he wanted to do, it absolutely blew my mind," Taylor told GACtv.com. Scott officially offered Taylor the first contract with his new independent label, Big Machine Records. Taylor was ecstatic to finally have a recording contract, and she was especially excited that it was with a new label, as she explained to GACtv.com. "That's always been my kind of thing. I've wanted to stir it up. I've always wanted people to say, 'Okay, she's doing things a little differently.'" Scott and Taylor were a perfect match and they didn't waste any time getting started.

Big Machine Records was up and running within a couple of months, and, in late Fall 2005, Taylor signed her recording contract in a special ceremony at the Country Music Hall of Fame in downtown Nashville. Signing that contract was a big moment for Taylor. "It's kind of like a wedding contract," Taylor joked. But Scott wasn't joking when he answered, "No, it's more binding." After the signing, Scott took Taylor and her family out for a celebratory dinner at The Palm restaurant. Taylor had just signed up for the ride of a lifetime and she was ready to enjoy it.

Once the celebration was over, Taylor and Scott got down to business in the recording studio. Taylor had kept plenty of the songs she'd written at Sony for herself, so she had lots of material to work with. Taylor presented all of them to her new label president, and Scott was absolutely in awe of her talent. "I've never seen anything like it, to be honest with you. There's something about her songwriting that's just extraordinary. She has this amazing filter. Everyday life comes in and it comes out Taylor Swift music. I've had the good fortune to be working with a lot of great songwriters. And I'll put her in the room with anybody," he told GACtv.com.

In the end, Taylor and Scott chose three songs that Taylor had written on her own and eight that she had cowritten during her time at Sony, including "Tim McGraw." "We played it for Scott, the president of my label, on a fluke—'Hey! Listen to this song I wrote called "Tim McGraw."' He looked at me and said, 'That's your first single.' I'm like, 'Well. *That's* how that works, then.' It never really occurred to me that the song would be so relatable," Taylor told

GACtv.com. It was very important to Taylor that her albums contained only music she had written, and Scott agreed completely. Especially since they'd agreed that the album would simply be called *Taylor Swift*—Taylor didn't want to put her name on anything that wasn't completely hers!

Once the songs were chosen, it was time to record. It took four months to finish the album, and the process wasn't without its ups and downs. Taylor liked the producers and writers she had been working with at Sony, especially her demo producer Nathan Chapman, and was a little thrown off by working with new people who didn't know and understand her, no matter how talented they were. "We switched [album] producers a bunch of times," Taylor explained to CMT.com. "Then, all of a sudden, it was, 'Okay, we're going to use this producer,' or, 'We're going to use that producer.' So I got to record with a bunch of really awesome producers in Nashville. But it didn't sound the way that it did with Nathan. He had never made an album before. He had just recorded demos. But the right chemistry hit. Finally my record label president said, 'OK, try some sides with Nathan.'"

In the end, Nathan produced all but one of the tracks on Taylor's debut and she couldn't have been happier with the final result.

Once the tracks were all recorded, Taylor's self-titled album still had to be mixed and the finishing touches, like the album cover and promotional materials, had to be added. Taylor tried to be patient, but she was anxious to present her masterpiece to the world. Scott began building the buzz about Taylor's debut all over town, and by June he felt the time was finally right to release her first single, "Tim McGraw." Taylor's life would never be the same.

☆ ☆ CHAPTER 6 ☆ ☆
The Online Country

After all her hard work in the studio, Taylor wanted the world to hear her album, but she had a long wait before the release date. Taylor has never been one to take it easy and she felt like she needed to do something productive while she was waiting for her album to drop. All of her friends at school were hooked on the online social networking site MySpace, and Taylor thought it might be a good idea to create a profile for herself as a country music artist. Lots of musicians, bands, and singers create profiles on the site so fans can sample their music and check in for concert dates and news. Fans can also request to be added as friends of the artist and leave comments and feedback. Taylor knew she and her friends liked to spend hours online checking out new music, so she thought MySpace was a great way to get in touch with potential fans. The only problem was that there just weren't very many country artists online and Taylor wasn't sure if anyone would even find her profile. Still, she was determined to at least give it a try.

Knowing the types of things that she and her friends checked out and responded to on MySpace, Taylor designed her profile. She wrote her biography in the first person, added all of the tracks from her album, pictures and video clips, a schedule of promotional events, and links to her official websites. She even added a girly pink floral background as the finishing touch. "I wrote it about who I am as a person. I have never been afraid to let people in to see that part of me, that I actually am a human being," Taylor explained to the *Tennessean*. After building her profile, Taylor began to watch it fanatically. She added all of her friends and classmates as MySpace friends and waited. Soon friends of friends began requesting to be her friend because they had clicked on her page and enjoyed her music. Taylor couldn't believe it. Every time she checked her page there were more and more friend requests waiting for her and more and more people had listened to her songs. "I'm a MySpace freak," Taylor admitted to GACtv.com. "I'm absolutely obsessed with it." Taylor was thrilled that people were responding so favorably to her music, especially people her own age. As she explained to the *Tennessean*, "It's cool because my fans are all ages. Of course, there are a lot of them that are my age. That is so flattering to me because I know how picky I am about music and how picky my friends are about music. They are ruthless. But if they like something, they are so passionate and loyal. That is why I am so happy to have fans that are my age."

As Taylor's popularity on MySpace grew, her fans began clamoring for their own copies of her catchy songs. Taylor had over 2 million hits on her profile before her debut album was even released. Since "Tim McGraw" hit the airways, it has been downloaded over 500,000 times and is one of only a handful of country singles to be certified Digital Gold. Taylor chalks it all up to her MySpace fan base, since it took a while for her single to break into country radio playlists. "I think MySpace has worked so well because I didn't want to make (my page) like every other artist's page, with a third-person bio that was completely not personal. Instead of doing that, I wrote a first-person bio about what I like and dislike. It is about what I am as a person, not my accomplishments. It lets them in and lets them know it's me running it, not a company. I love the fact that people my age are paying attention to my music. I know how my friends and I look at music and address music, either they love something or don't like it at all," she explained to the *Modesto Bee*. Once *Taylor Swift* hit store shelves, the number of Taylor's MySpace friends shot through the roof as fans searched the Internet for more information on their favorite new singer.

Taylor's openness and personal approach on her profile helps fans feel like they really know her and are important to her—and they are. Taylor checks her page daily and tries to answer as many fan e-mails as possible. Before her album was released and her life became a whirlwind, Taylor would respond to about one hundred e-mails and postings per day. Andrea and Scott Swift would often have to force Taylor to turn off her computer and go to bed at night, and Taylor still felt she wasn't doing enough to respond to her fans. As she explained to GACtv.com, "My fans have done so much for me and have been pulling for me from the very beginning. It kills me that I can't go out to every single person in some way and say thank you so much and shake their hand." Her fans really relate to Taylor's songs and want to share with her how much her music has touched them. "They come on [MySpace] and tell their life story or why this song has meant so much to them. They're sharing their lives with Taylor," Andrea told GACtv.com.

The country music industry certainly took notice when teenage Taylor burst onto the scene with a ready-made fan base that already knew all of the words to her songs. The number of people Taylor had connected with using only her home computer blew the studios away. Lots of older music executives were especially puzzled, but Taylor knew exactly why MySpace had worked so well for her. As she explained to the *Tennessean,* "I nurtured it and really paid attention to it, like it was something important and not just a marketing tool." And Taylor wasn't just appealing to the traditional country fans—she was introducing a whole new generation to the genre, something country's bigwigs had been struggling to do for quite a while. "I think one of the cool things about this is that MySpace is one of the main reasons I'm here, along with radio and word of mouth. And MySpace is pretty much a younger thing, at the moment . . . So yeah, definitely, it's bringing a completely different audience to country music. And I am so grateful for that. I don't know what I did to make that happen, because everybody was talking about it. I would go to [Country Radio Seminar] before I was ever signed to a record deal, and I would listen to people say, 'Someone needs to bring in that younger demographic.' And what I'm hearing is that we've done that, and we kind of stumbled upon it. I wasn't trying to be exclusive as to who would like it," Taylor told *Entertainment Weekly.*

For Taylor, who had grown up with computers and the Internet, using her computer to access music is second nature, and she feels that kids her age are more open-minded about trying out new and different types of music since they can download just about any song out there for under a dollar. "In this day of iPods and digital and Internet and the fact people can go get any music they want with the click of a button, I really think there are less boundaries and the lines are more blurred between genres. And I think that's a beautiful thing," Taylor told the *Ontario Star.*

It's been almost four years since Taylor's MySpace profile went up at myspace.com/TaylorSwift and she is still dominating the social networking site. She is ranked number 15 for the most MySpace visits in all genres of music and is number one for the number of visits for a country artist, outdistancing other country artists by millions of hits. Fans have streamed songs off of her profile more than 229 million times. Radio airplay is great, but with Taylor's fans coming directly to her MySpace page for music, it isn't as necessary as it once was. The Internet has completely revolutionized the music business for most genres of music—country is just one of the last genres to realize it. "People haven't fallen out of love with music, they've just fallen in love with new ways to use it," Scott Borchetta said to *HonkeyTonk* magazine. And that's just fine with Taylor. She loves being so accessible to her fans, and can't wait for MySpace to develop new ways for her and other musicians to get their music out there.

☆ ☆ CHAPTER 7 ☆ ☆

Taylor and Tim McGraw

It took Taylor forever to fall asleep on the night of June 18, 2006. The next day, June 19, her debut single "Tim McGraw" was going to be officially released. It had been up on her MySpace page for months and fans loved it, but Taylor was still nervous. She was also excited to hear herself on the radio, and hoped that Nashville's radio stations wouldn't bash all of her hard work on the air. Little did she know that she had nothing to worry about.

"Tim McGraw" hit the airwaves the next day and immediately began racing up the Billboard Hot Digital Songs chart, which includes music from all genres. It would eventually peak at number 33 on that chart—which is pretty high for a country single. It took a little longer for "Tim McGraw" to really break into the notoriously tight country radio rotations. Country fans are known for being a little resistant to accepting new artists, but once they do, an artist is usually in for life. Scott warned Taylor it might take some time, so she tried to be patient. The first time Taylor heard her song on the radio, she was in her car with friends and family. A Nashville radio station played two new singles and then asked listeners to vote for their favorites. One was "Tim McGraw" and the other, ironically, was a new song by Tim's wife, Faith Hill. Faith is a well-established country superstar and Taylor thought she would lose, but, to her surprise, fans liked her song best! But Faith probably didn't mind losing to a song with her husband's name in the title.

Luckily, Taylor was much too busy to worry about her chart standings. As soon as school let out, she set out on a six-month-long radio tour to promote "Tim McGraw" and her debut album, *Taylor Swift*. "Radio tours for most artists last six weeks. Mine lasted six months. That's because I wanted it to. I wanted to meet every single one of the people that was helping me out," she explained to CMT.com. Taylor wasn't at all shy about getting into every radio station and convincing DJs that her music was worth playing. For the most part, Taylor and her genuine enthusiasm charmed the DJs, and she made friends at every station she stopped into. Being on the road was grueling, but Taylor cherished every minute of it—after all, she'd been working toward having an album to promote since she was ten years old—and she wasn't about to complain.

Taylor did take a break from the tour in October 2006, when Big Machine Records finally released *Taylor Swift*. It was a very big and emotional moment for Taylor, and it was definitely the highlight of her year. She was in New York City for the big day and was so excited that she went out and bought a copy of her own album that afternoon. Then she went home to Nashville for a few days to celebrate with her family and visit her friends. Taylor had decided to begin homeschooling so she could throw herself into her music career, but she missed seeing her friends every day, especially her best friend, Abigail. But they were all so happy for her that they almost didn't mind her being gone so much—and of course they were some of the first people to run out and buy *Taylor Swift*.

Thanks to the momentum Taylor had built up promoting "Tim McGraw," her album sold steadily and began climbing the Billboard charts. It went gold by February 2007, only four short months after its release. Sony BMI threw their then-favorite songwriter a party so that Taylor could accept her gold album plaque in style. Taylor wore a sparkling gold dress in honor of the occasion and celebrated with a mix of Nashville music industry insiders, Hendersonville High School students and teachers, and family and close friends. It wasn't just the first gold album for Taylor—it was also the first gold album for Big Machine Records and Nathan Chapman, Taylor's producer. Scott Borchetta, Big Machine's president, was elated by the achievement, but he was also keeping his fingers crossed for more. He wore a platinum tie to the event to symbolize the next milestone he was hoping Taylor would achieve.

With her album doing well, "Tim McGraw" began to get a lot more airplay and continued creeping up the charts. It eventually reached number 6 on Billboard's Hot Country Songs chart, number

43 on Billboard's Pop 100 chart, and number 40 on the Billboard Hot 100 chart. Taylor's single was achieving something that few country songs ever do; it was being embraced by the music world outside of the country scene. "I think the reason why 'Tim McGraw' worked out was it was reminiscent, and it was thinking about a relationship that you had and then lost. I think one of the most powerful human emotions is what should have been and wasn't. I think everyone can relate to that. That was a really good first song to start out on, just because a lot of people can relate to wanting what you can't have," Taylor told *Entertainment Weekly*.

It seemed like the time was right to spin another single off the album, and Scott Borchetta thought "Teardrops On My Guitar" was the perfect choice. As soon as it was released, "Teardrops" shot up the charts, eventually hitting number 2 on the Billboard Hot Country Songs chart in August, number 11 on the Billboard Hot Digital Songs chart and the Pop 100 charts, number 14 on the Billboard Hot 100 chart, and number 5 on the Billboard Hot Adult Contemporary chart. In January 2008, "Teardrops

On My Guitar" became the fourth digital platinum single in country music history, meaning that over 1 million people had downloaded the single. Carrie Underwood, Rascal Flatts, and the Dixie Chicks are the only other artists to ever achieve that distinction. The popularity of "Teardrops" brought fame to someone in addition to Taylor—her one-time crush, Drew Hardwick. He was probably pretty surprised to hear his own name coming out of the radio. Other Hendersonville residents recognized his name, too, and soon Hendersonville High students were buying Taylor's album just to see if there were any songs about them on it. "The funny thing is, there are so many people in the town where I live, Hendersonville, that think they do have a song written about 'em. You go out into this big world and you go on tour with all these people, and you go back and it's still a small town and they still gossip about it. I think it's one of everybody's favorite things to talk about—who my songs are written about. There are definitely a few more people who think that I've written songs about them than there actually are," Taylor laughingly told *Entertainment Weekly*.

Shortly after the release of her second single, in June 2007, Taylor and her family drove to downtown Nashville to the convention center for what they thought was another gold record presentation ceremony. Taylor's debut album had gone gold in February and she had already been presented with one gold album, so she was a little confused as to why there was going to be a second ceremony. Little did Taylor know that she was in for a big surprise. During the ceremony, instead of a gold plaque, a representative from the Recording Industry Association of America handed her a platinum plaque, meaning that her album had sold over 1 million copies. When she saw the plaque, she turned to Scott Borchetta, her label president and the organizer of the ceremony, and shouted, "Scott, you liar!" It was quite the feat for Scott to pull one over on Taylor, who is always on top of everything having to do with her career. "I would have been happy to get another gold record, but it was a platinum record. It's the most beautiful thing that I think I've ever seen my life. When I was a little kid, I went to a Kenny Chesney concert and just thought,

'If I can have a platinum album, I'll be set and I'll be satisfied with what I've done.' Here it is and it's such an amazing feeling," Taylor gushed to shoutmouth. com. "It's just crazy that in just under eight months we were able to go platinum. Eight months is not a very long time at all. Seeing how people have rallied behind me like this, it's breathtaking, really. I can't comprehend that a million people are out there flying my flag and being awesome and buying my record." Scott Borchetta wasn't surprised, though—he was convinced that going platinum in eight months was just the beginning for Big Machine Records's star, and counted on Taylor's debut going triple platinum before her second album dropped in 2008. (His prediction came true in late April 2008, just in time for Taylor to announce the news on April 29 when she appeared on *Good Morning America*.)

Taylor released her third single, "Our Song," in the fall of 2007, and it quickly became the biggest hit from her first record, topping the Billboard Hot Country Song chart before the end of 2007. It was Taylor's first number 1 single and her third top 10 single in one year! "Our Song" also hit number 15 on the Billboard Hot Digital Songs chart in 2007. It went gold in January 2008, and also hit number 16 on the Billboard Hot 100 chart and number 24 on the Billboard Pop 100 chart in February 2008. "Our Song" seems to be a favorite with fans, and its popularity certainly helped propel *Taylor Swift* even further up the charts.

By the end of 2007, Taylor had hit two more very important musical milestones—her debut album had gone double platinum, selling over 2 million copies, and had hit number 1 on Billboard's Top Country chart, making country music history. Taylor was officially the only female country music artist to ever write or cowrite all of the songs on a double-platinum, number 1 debut album! Her album spent more than sixty-six consecutive weeks on the Top Country chart and more than twelve straight weeks in the number 1 spot. Taylor was officially the breakout country star of 2007, and while her album and singles had been burning up the charts, Taylor had spent most of that year out on tour performing and thanking her fans for helping make her number 1.

☆ ☆ CHAPTER 8 ☆ ☆
Hitting the Road

Going on tour was a dream come true for Taylor. She got to perform and introduce her music to new fans. "I've learned that when you write a song, not everyone hears it right away. I have to introduce myself and play it for one person at a time, and when I want to sell 500,000 albums, I have to meet 500,000 people," Taylor told the *Denver Westword*. She started out with a six-month radio tour in 2006 to promote "Tim McGraw." This did a lot to help boost the amount of playtime her single got on the radio, but it didn't give Taylor many chances to perform live, so she was thrilled when Rascal Flatts asked her to join them on tour in 2006.

Rascal Flatts's Me and My Gang tour was one of the hottest tickets of 2006. The country trio, known for its tight harmonies and mix of pop, country, and rock, is made up of Gary LeVox, Jay DeMarcus, and

Joe Don Rooney. The group was on tour to promote their third number 1 album, *Me and My Gang*, and they sold out most of their performances. Taylor joined the tour in October 2006 and stayed with the band through the end of the year. Taylor played her heart out every night, and learned a lot about touring from the seasoned veterans, including what it felt like to have fans really treat her like a star. "I'm still in the 'Oh-my-gosh-this-is-really-happening' phase. After all these concerts that I do, people line up and want me to sign things. I still haven't been able to grasp the fact that if I sign a piece of paper, it might mean something to somebody," Taylor told CMT.com. It was the perfect first tour for Taylor and it set the tone for her future travels.

After spending Christmas at home with her family, Taylor hit the road again in 2007, opening for country legend George Strait for two-and-a-half months. George Strait was a country superstar before Taylor was even born. He has had over fifty number 1 hits and has sold more than 62 million copies of his thirteen multi-platinum, thirty platinum, and thirty-three gold albums! "With George Strait, I feel I'm lucky to be in front of a more traditional country audience," Taylor told CMT.com. The crowd's respect for Strait and his music, she told CMT.com, was "like religion." After getting the chance to experience that level of intense fan devotion, Taylor was ready to experience another one of country music's legendary traditions.

On April 14, 2007, Taylor stepped out onto country music's most famous stage at the Grand Ole Opry. The tradition of the Grand Ole Opry started in 1925 as live Saturday-night broadcasts from the Ryman Auditorium for WSM Radio. The Opry has introduced America to most of country music's greats, and an appearance there is a sure sign that an artist has finally made it. Wearing a short, teal, sequined dress, Taylor gave a powerful performance. She was humbled to sing on the same stage which Dolly Parton, Patsy Cline, Hank Williams, and Johnny Cash, among others, had made their own.

Later in 2007, Taylor set out on a tour that was more like being at a summer camp than work. She joined Jack Ingram, Kellie Pickler, and headliner Brad Paisley on Brad's Bonfires and Amplifiers tour for about five months. Brad Paisley personally requested Taylor for his tour after hearing her album. As he told *Entertainment Weekly*, "Taylor Swift was one that I called my manager when I heard her album and said, 'We have to get her out on tour.' And for her to have written that record at 16, it's crazy how good it is. I figured I'd hear it and think, 'Well, it's good for 16'—but it's just flat-out good for any age." Brad wasn't disappointed by his decision to put Taylor on the tour. Taylor was seventeen at the time. Kellie Pickler was the closest to her in age, at twenty-one. Brad Paisley was thirty-four; Jack Ingram was thirty-six. But Taylor fit right in with everyone, despite the differences in their ages. Taylor and Kellie became close friends and the two girls had a fantastic time goofing around and playing pranks offstage. Brad is a notorious prankster, but Kellie and Taylor decided to get him before he had the opportunity to play a prank on either of them. "We pranked him first, all the opening acts. You can go on MySpace and watch it. You know how his single is called 'Ticks'? I went online and I ordered these giant tick costumes—like big, giant sumo-wrestler-looking tick costumes—

82

and me and Kellie dressed up in them and ran out on stage and started dancing all around him. And then Jack Ingram, the other opening act, came out in this white exterminator suit halfway through the song, with a sprayer, and proceeded to kill us on stage," Taylor told *Entertainment Weekly*. The high-energy tour was a hit with Taylor's fans, most of whom are also fans of the other acts.

Taylor did take a brief break from the Bonfires and Amplifiers tour to perform a few shows with Kenny Chesney in June 2007. Sugarland was one of his other opening acts, and Taylor loves them. Like Jennifer Nettles, Sugarland's powerhouse singer, Taylor likes performing covers of unexpected songs, like Beyoncé's "Irreplaceable." Taylor also learned a lot about bantering with a crowd and really working the stage from watching Sugarland and Kenny Chesney.

After her time on the road with Kenny, another of Taylor's personal dreams came true. She got to go on tour with Tim McGraw and Faith Hill! It was a short engagement, but it was a huge thrill for Taylor. Tim and Faith are both country megastars whose music has inspired millions of fans. They didn't have an opening act on their Soul2Soul tour, so Taylor performed as a special guest. Taylor's fans definitely enjoyed getting to see her sing "Tim McGraw" while sharing the stage with him.

Taylor finished off 2007 by touring with Brad Paisley again. By November, when the tour finally wrapped, Taylor had been on the road for almost a solid year. "There's definitely a feeling of it all being a blur every once in a while," Taylor told the *Ontario Star*. But it was all worth it. The touring helped Taylor hone her performance skills and gave her a chance to personally thank the fans who had supported her from the beginning. It also gave her an opportunity to see a lot of different places. As she told the *Ontario Star*, "It definitely rounds you out as a human being . . . I feel like I've already gone to college . . . as far as being away from home, having to learn how to survive, having to learn so many different things about the (music) industry and meeting different people you've never met before."

Taylor had always been a mature teenager, but her mother still accompanies her when she's on the road while her father stays home with Austin, Taylor's brother. "It's a lot of work helping Tay pursue a music career, but it's a lot of fun, too," Andrea told searay.com. Mother and daughter manage to get along well on the road, as Taylor explained to GACtv.com. "This is going to sound horrible but the only real argument that I have with my mom is, the temperature on the tour bus. She likes it freezing, and I don't. I like the bus really, really hot. So usually, she'll turn the bus temperature all the way down to 65, and be like, 'Taylor! You've got to stop turning it up!' and then I'll be like, 'Okay Mom.' When she turns around to walk away I'll turn it back to 80. Then she'll come back and be like, 'Taylor!' So those are the only real arguments that we get in. My mom and I really get along and my dad and I get along really well so it's gotten to the point where all we argue about is stupid stuff."

For 2008, Big Machine Records bought their star a brand-new, custom tour bus—it even has a treadmill in it! And Taylor has stocked it with all of her favorite things. "Some of my must-have items are makeup—I love makeup," Taylor told

GACtv.com. "It's not that I absolutely need it, but I really like it. I think it's fun. It's like art class. Also I like my cell phone, just because I like keeping in touch with people. I always have to be knowing exactly what's going on with my career at that moment. I'm always bothering my record label—'Hey! What's going on today? What are we working on?' I am really annoying. Also, I love keeping in touch with my friends. I have an iPod that I always take with me on the road. Let's see, what else do I take on the road with me a lot? I have these boots that have skulls on them, and then they have a pink bow on the top of the skull. They are really cute. They are Liberty boots and I always take them everywhere with me when I travel."

At the beginning of 2008, Taylor went back on the road. She joined Alan Jackson for his Like Red on a Rose tour in January and February. Alan Jackson is another country legend that Taylor probably picked up some amazing performance tips from. He's released sixteen albums, sold over 50 million copies of his albums, and has had thirty-four number 1 songs, twenty-one of which he wrote.

Who knows—maybe Taylor will write a song with Alan Jackson someday! After that, Taylor headed up to Canada for a five-city run in March with her old buddies Rascal Flatts. Even though she loved going on tour with other amazing country acts, Taylor still hoped to someday headline her own tour. She couldn't wait to put everything she'd learned while traveling with all of these country superstars to good use!

In 2007 and 2008, Taylor did take some time off from touring to make a few special appearances, like performing on the season finale of *America's Got Talent* on August 21, 2007. Fourteen-year-old finalist Julienne Irwin requested to sing a duet with Taylor for the live telecast. "Taylor Swift is a huge inspiration to me! She is not only a great singer, she's a great songwriter as well, and it is truly an honor to have the opportunity to perform with her on stage. I know I'm not the only one inspired by her, and I hope my performance makes her proud!" Julienne told GACtv.com. Each of the finalists got to sing with the performer of their choice, and Taylor was honored to be asked. "I can't wait to sing with Julienne on *America's Got Talent*! She's such a sweetheart, and I'm so unbelievably honored that she chose me as her duet choice. She's got such a powerful voice and her story is so endearing," Taylor told GACtv.com. Unfortunately, Julienne didn't win, but she did have a blast performing with her favorite singer. In addition to appearing on television shows and at concerts, Taylor also got to perform at a number of award shows—and she even managed to win a few awards in the process!

CHAPTER 9

Video Heaven

Taylor's schedule was hectic, but she loved it that way. So in between tour dates and performing at special events, Taylor filmed her first music videos. With all of the radio play Taylor was getting, she wasn't too worried about her music videos getting on the air on CMT and GAC, the two television channels devoted to country music. It wasn't difficult for Taylor to get in the groove of filming a video. After all, she is a natural born performer!

The first video that Taylor filmed was for the song "Tim McGraw." The concept for the video was simple—two young teenagers remembering the love they had once shared. It cut between Taylor singing by a lake, a handsome boy driving in his pickup truck, and scenes of the two of them together in the past. By the end of the video, the boy finds a letter from Taylor waiting for him. The video's storyline mimics the story Taylor tells in the song and incorporates plenty of the details she sings about. The actor in the video even looked a lot like the boy Taylor wrote the song about! "[The actor's] name is Clayton Collins, and I think that he lives in L.A. right now. He was a really sweet guy but definitely not my boyfriend . . . But the guy that 'Tim McGraw' was written about looked a lot like the guy we picked for the video. That was done on purpose. He was really tall with dark hair," Taylor explained to GACtv.com. Fans loved the video and were soon requesting it on video countdowns. The video eventually climbed the charts to hit number 1 on CMT's video charts and then made CMT's top videos of 2007 at number 20. It also set a record by appearing for thirty consecutive weeks on GAC's fan-voted weekly Top 20 music countdown show.

When it came time to record her second music video, for "Teardrops On My Guitar," Taylor and her director decided to follow the same formula that had worked the first time. In "Teardrops On My Guitar," Taylor has a crush on a boy named Drew who doesn't know about or reciprocate her feelings, and Taylor and the director wanted the video to tell that story. Luckily, Taylor found the perfect boy at one of her concerts in California. Tyler Hilton, a singer and actor who had appeared on the hit show *One Tree Hill* and in films like *Walk the Line*, had admitted he was a Taylor fan in a magazine article. When Taylor saw that, she had her manager send him tickets to a show. "I found out he was a fan of my music and he came to my show. I met him in the 'meet and greet' line, and we became friends. He came onstage with me at the show, and I asked him in front of the crowd, 'Do you want to be in my video?' and he said, 'Yeah!'" Taylor told *Country Standard Time*.

Tyler was a perfect choice to play Drew. With his tousled hair and chiseled features, he was instantly believable as the high school hotshot who didn't notice that his beautiful best friend liked him. The video was set in a high school and cut between scenes of Taylor and "Drew" goofing off with scenes of Taylor, dressed in a beautiful gown, lying alone on her bed holding her guitar. Taylor and Tyler had a blast filming together and are still friends. He loves going to her shows, and, whenever he's there, she invites him up onstage to sing with her. The video for "Teardrops On My Guitar" did incredibly well on the country channels CMT and GAC, but it also made it into the Top 20 countdown on VH1 and went into rotation on notoriously anti-country MTV. Taylor had her first crossover video hit—and it was only her second single! It was even voted the number 10 video for all of 2007 on CMT.

For the video for "Our Song," Taylor decided to change things up and skip casting a boy altogether! It opens with Taylor, wearing shorts and a tank top with her hair straightened, painting her toenails and chatting on the phone, and cuts between that and Taylor in several other scenes. In one, she is wearing a blue dress with a full skirt and singing on a porch. In another, she is wearing a bright orange floor-length gown and lying in a bed of multicolored roses, and in the last scene, she's in a little black dress, rocking out with her entire band. In the last scene, Taylor is strumming a brand-new guitar that's as dressed up as she is—the entire face is covered in glittering rhinestones! Taylor's fans began voting for the video immediately. After only a few weeks, "Our Song" made it to number 1 on both CMT and GAC.

But her music videos weren't Taylor's first television appearances. In the summer of 2006, Taylor's pursuit of stardom was the subject of a debut series called *GAC Short Cuts* that aired on the Great American Country channel. The series gave Taylor's fans a chance to see the young singer at home, at school, hanging out with her friends, and promoting her album. The crew followed Taylor into her high school to watch her perform a song called "I'd Lie" that she'd just written for the school talent show, into the studio for a recording session, to New York City to perform on *Good Morning America*, to the concert where she was opening for George Strait, and at home on a rare day off with her family. The six-episode series was the perfect way to introduce spunky Taylor to fans of country music, and it helped make Taylor more comfortable on camera. Her honesty, enthusiasm, and tendency to wear her heart on her sleeve endeared her to fans. Taylor was winning fans left and right!

☆☆ CHAPTER 10 ☆☆
A Little Recognition

There is nothing more satisfying for musicians than to be recognized for their work by their peers and fans at an awards show. The first year that Taylor was eligible for any awards was 2007, and once nominations were announced for all of the major country music awards, Taylor kept a running countdown in her head of the upcoming shows. She was nervous and excited and absolutely thrilled to be nominated for any awards.

Her first big show was the 2007 CMT Music Awards on April 16 at Belmont University's Curb Event Center. Taylor was nominated in two categories: the Buckle Breakthrough Video of the Year award and the Female Video of the Year award, both for "Tim McGraw," though she was edged out of the final nominee list for Female Video of the Year. Taylor arrived at the awards show wearing a beautiful white dress with graduated silver sequins covering the bodice and skirt, nervous to find out whether or not she had won. Taylor had tried not to get her hopes up too high, so she was shocked when she heard her name announced as the winner of the Breakthrough Video award! She ran up to the podium, flushed with excitement, and accepted her trophy from 2006's winner, fellow country superstar Carrie Underwood. "I cannot believe this is happening right now. This is for my MySpace people and the fans," Taylor said, holding up her trophy. Taylor didn't win the Female Video of the Year award, but she didn't mind at all. "The highlight of my career so far has been winning the CMT Breakthrough Video of the Year award. It's a fan-voted awards show, so I don't see any greater honor than winning an award that was voted on by fans. It was for my first video that I ever put out ['Tim McGraw'], and I'll never forget the feeling of just running . . . bolting up to that stage. It was just the most amazing feeling," Taylor explained to theboot.com in 2007. Since it was her first award, it was extra special to Taylor, as she told the *Tennessean*. "I can't explain the feeling.

(1) Stunning in red at the 4th Annual Academy of Country Music Awards.

(1) Taylor acting as NHL spokesperson at an LA Kings hockey game.
(2) Taylor and fellow singer Colbie Caillat at the AMAs.

(3) Taylor and Zac Efron pose on the red carpet at the Australian premiere of *17 Again*. (4) Taylor performs the national anthem at the 2008 MLB World Series. (5) On stage with buddy Miley Cyrus at the Grammys.

(1) Looking cute in a belted wool trench on the streets of NYC. (2) Hanging with LeAnn Rimes at the CMAs. (3) On the set of *CSI*.

(4) Taylor with Ryan Tedder and Kelly Clarkson at the Grammy Salute to Industry Icons party. (5) Signing autographs for her fans.

(1) Watching the ball drop in Times Square on New Year's Eve with Lionel Richie, Ryan Seacrest, and Demi Lovato. (2) Taylor signs a guitar for MusiCares Signings.

(3) Taylor and Diddy backstage during the final episode of MTV's *TRL*. (4) Looking angelic at the CMA's Artist of the Decade show. (5) Taylor and Miley at the world premiere of *Hannah Montana: The Movie*.

(1) Taylor posing for the cameras with her CMA awards. (2) Looking rock star glam on stage!

I had never been nominated for anything before. I had won nothing before, literally nothing. To have my name called, I didn't know what that was like. I didn't think I was going to get it. When my name was called, I just ran up to the stage at, like, 100 miles an hour." That night and that award will probably always be especially important to Taylor, since that was the night when she really felt that she had made it in country music.

For her next awards show, the Academy of Country Music Awards in Las Vegas, Nevada, on May 15, 2007, Taylor was nominated for Top New Female Vocalist. She was also on deck to perform her single, "Tim McGraw," for a packed venue full of country music superstars and legends, including Tim McGraw himself. "It was unbelievable, I was performing on stage and it was just me and my guitar. After my song, I stepped down and said, 'Hi, I'm Taylor.'" Taylor told the *Modesto Bee*. Taylor lost to Carrie Underwood that night, but it would always be special to Taylor, anyway, because she finally got to meet the man whose music had inspired her first hit single. Plus, this was probably where Tim got the idea to invite Taylor to go on tour with him later that year!

On October 16, 2007, Taylor won a very prestigious award that very few stars are ever even nominated for—the Songwriter/Artist of the Year award from the Nashville Songwriters Association International. She actually tied with Alan Jackson for the award, and they were both honored that night. Taylor was the youngest artist to ever win the award and she didn't mind sharing the spotlight at all! "I am just freaking out. I'm so excited because I got a publishing deal when I was 14 and every single day was devoted to writing songs. And it was before I got a record deal, it was before any of this started. I was a songwriter in town. And the fact that this award is voted on by my songwriter peers—I don't even know how to explain how honored I feel. I mean, I was sitting at the table and they called Alan Jackson's name and I'm just like, 'Oh my God! That's awesome!' And then all of the sudden they say my name and I'm like, 'What happened?' I'm so humbled by this experience. It's just so unbelievable," Taylor told GACtv.com. Alan was so impressed by his cowinner that he invited Taylor to open for him on his next tour, which turned out to be almost as exciting for Taylor as it was to win the award!

But nothing up to that point could top the next award Taylor received. On November 7, 2007, Taylor attended the Country Music Association Awards at the Sommet Center in Nashville, Tennessee. Taylor wore a stunning, metallic gold dress with a fitted bodice and a full, cascading skirt. The event was televised nationally on ABC, and Taylor got the chance to perform her third single, "Our Song," for the crowd. She changed into the short black sequined dress, black tights, and long black gloves that she had worn in her music video for the same song, and strummed along on her rhinestone-covered guitar as she sang her heart out. The crowd was blown away by her performance, but Taylor was blown away when her name was announced as the winner of the prestigious Horizon Award. The Horizon Award is always given to a new country singer or group that has made a lasting impact on the industry. "I can't even believe this; this is definitely the highlight of my senior year," Taylor said as she accepted her trophy.

It was a huge honor to win that award, and Taylor was completely humbled by her success.

Taylor was also nominated for Favorite Female Country Artist at the American Music Awards, but she lost to Carrie Underwood on November 18, 2007. Taylor was just excited to have been nominated and hadn't expected to win, since she had some pretty stiff competition from Martina McBride and Carrie Underwood. Taylor looked adorable that night, though, wearing a short, black, sixties-inspired dress accented along the neck and front with metallic studs. She paired the dress with her favorite pair of black cowboy boots and enjoyed getting the chance to hang out in Los Angeles before and after the show.

Taylor received her most exciting nomination of the year bright and early on the morning of December 6, 2007. At only seventeen years old, Taylor was the youngest artist on the stage at the 50th Annual Grammy nomination announcement press conference. She was sharing the spotlight that morning with some pretty illustrious company, including Dave Grohl and Taylor Hawkins of the

Foo Fighters, Fergie, Akon, Quincy Jones, Linkin Park, and George Lopez. "I'm starstruck," Taylor admitted to *People*. She was very honored to be asked to help present the nominations for the biggest awards ceremony in the music industry.

The Grammy Awards encompass every genre of music, from country to hip-hop to pop to indie rock, making these nominations some of the most coveted. There are specific categories for every genre, and a few awards that acts from every genre compete for, such as Best New Artist. Ready to shine that morning, Taylor wore a simple, black dress and read off her assigned nominations with her usual bubbly enthusiasm. Then Dave Grohl and Taylor Hawkins of the quirky rock group the Foo Fighters took the podium to announce the nominees for Best New Artist. Taylor was shocked to hear Dave announce her name. She instantly squealed with excitement, rushed over to Dave Grohl and Taylor Hawkins, and gave them both huge hugs. "Don't worry, Taylor, you got it in the bag," Dave said as he hugged her back. All of the veteran musicians onstage were charmed by Taylor's enthusiasm. George Lopez got so caught up in the moment that he gave her a big hug, too. "I've always been a hugger. I honestly did not think I was going to get nominated, so when they said my name I just felt like hugging somebody. I'm glad that everyone started hugging. If we all hugged more, the world would be a better place," Taylor told *People*. After everyone shared a laugh and finished hugging, they got on with the nominations, but Taylor was still shocked by her nomination. "It absolutely blows me away that these people even know my name and can pronounce it right," Taylor told theboot.com.

Taylor was especially pleased to be nominated for the Best New Artist award, since many of the previous winners have gone on to have some of the most successful careers in music, including The Beatles, Alicia Keys, Sheryl Crow, Taylor's idol LeAnn Rimes, and 2007's winner, Taylor's friend Carrie Underwood. "It's so unbelievable. That's an all-genre category, and there's certainly no obligation to have a country artist in the category," Taylor told the *Houston Chronicle*.

The 50th annual Grammy Awards were held at the Staples Center in Los Angeles on the night of

February 10, 2008, and were broadcast live on CBS. Taylor looked stunning as she worked the red carpet wearing a strapless purple gown with a flowing skirt and leaf details. Her blond, corkscrew curls hung loosely down her back and she positively glowed with anticipation. Unfortunately for Taylor, British singer Amy Winehouse took home the award that night, but Taylor was thrilled just to have been a part of the prestigious award show. She did get the chance to make her debut in front of the Grammy audience that night when she appeared as a presenter alongside Juanes for the Best Rap Song Collaboration. Taylor joked with her copresenter and charmed the crowd. Then she presented the award to Rihanna and Jay-Z for "Umbrella," which also happened to be one of Taylor's favorite songs to cover at her concerts!

In 2008, Taylor was also named Billboard's Top Country Artist and Hot Country Songwriter of 2008. That one had been an easy choice, though, in a way. After all, Taylor had been the best-selling country music artist of the year! She also ranked seventh on Nielsen SoundScan Canada's top 10 artists of 2008, and her two albums were number

1 and number 2 on the 2008 Year-End Canadian Country Albums Chart. Good to know her appeal crosses the border!

In October 2008, Taylor got an award of a different sort. She was chosen to sing the Star-Spangled Banner at Game Three of the World Series in Philadelphia. Taylor and her father were both Phillies fans anyway, and had been ever since their early days in Pennsylvania. But for Taylor there was extra excitement. "I love it when people freak out when they win something," she told *Rolling Stone*, "and it's crazy because I actually used to sing the National Anthem for the Reading Phillies, which is their minor league team, and a lot of the members of the Philadelphia Phillies now were on that minor league team when I sang that anthem years and years and years ago." Needless to say, she was thrilled when the Phillies wound up winning the World Series against the Tampa Bay Rays! "I was watching and my dad and I were sitting there crying," she admitted, "especially during the last throw of the game."

☆☆ CHAPTER 11 ☆☆
A Christmas Gift

Taylor has always loved Christmas, but she got into the spirit extra early in 2007 when she recorded her holiday album, *Sounds of the Season: The Taylor Swift Holiday Collection* in July. Taylor wrote a few original holiday tunes, but also put her own spin on classics like "Silent Night," "Santa Baby," and "White Christmas." The album was released exclusively in Target stores on October 14, 2007, and it was the best Christmas gift Taylor could have given her eager fans.

The holiday album did very well. It hit number 46 on the Billboard 200 chart and number 14 on Billboard's Top Country Albums chart. Singles from the album also did fairly well on Billboard's Hot Country Songs chart. "White Christmas" hit number 59, "Silent Night" peaked at number 54, Taylor's original composition "Christmases When

You Were Mine" made it to number 48, the ever popular "Santa Baby" hit number 43, and "Last Christmas" made it all the way to number 28. Not bad for a holiday album sold in only one chain store!

In addition to *Sounds of the Season*, Taylor released a second special album on November 6, 2007—*Taylor Swift: Deluxe Limited Edition*. Taylor was itching to give her fans new music, but her label wanted her to wait a little longer before releasing her next album. As a compromise, they repackaged her debut album with some amazing extras and a few new songs. As Taylor explained to theboot.com, "The album has been out for a year, but it's too early to put out the second studio album. But we wanted to give [the fans] more music. So this was an opportunity to put out three new songs and a bunch of exclusive content. I actually edited a home movie on my laptop, and it's on there as a special feature. There's my first phone conversation with Tim McGraw, all my music videos and a bunch of concert footage. The [new] songs are demos that I wrote when I was 15, trying to get a record deal."

The new songs on the album are "Invisible," a song about a girl who is in love with a boy who is in love with another girl who doesn't know he exists; "A Perfectly Good Heart," a bittersweet song about suffering through a first heartbreak; and "I'm Only Me When I'm With You," an upbeat, happy song about young love and how all-consuming it can be. Taylor wrote all three of the bonus songs and, while they hadn't made it onto her album originally, they had been good enough to help land her the record deal with Big Machine Records. Fans loved the bonus material and these three extra songs were some of the most downloaded on iTunes. Taylor was very glad that those three songs got a second life with the release of the bonus album, as all three were very personal tunes that she had always wanted to share with her fans.

The following summer, Taylor released another exclusive album. *Beautiful Eyes* debuted on July 15, 2008, and was sold exclusively at Wal-Mart stores around the country. The CD featured six tracks, including an alternate version of "Should've Said No," the radio version of "Picture To Burn," the energetic "I'm Only Me When I'm With You," and an acoustic version of "Teardrops On My Guitar." But the CD also had two new songs: the title track, "Beautiful Eyes," which was a simple, sweet love song and the bold, upbeat "I Heart?" about the aftermath of a breakup. An accompanying DVD contained music videos for all six songs, plus a twenty-two-minute special on the making of the "Picture To Burn" video, a fifteen-minute interview for GAC's Best New Artist Special, and Taylor's performance of "Should've Said No" from the 2008 ACM Awards.

In its first week, *Beautiful Eyes* sold 45,000 copies, putting it at number 1 on Billboard's Top Country Albums chart and number 9 on the Billboard 200. Taylor's self-titled debut album was at number 2 on the Top Country Albums chart the same week, which made Taylor the first solo artist to hold those top two positions since her role model LeAnn Rimes did it in 1997. Clearly Taylor had chosen a good person to pattern her career after!

Taylor's fans were thrilled with *Beautiful Eyes*. It whetted their appetites for the release of Taylor's second new album, which was exactly what she had hoped for. At the same time, it gave fans new songs and new versions of old songs so they had something to add to their growing Taylor Swift collection while waiting for the new album to drop. It was a great way for Taylor to make her fans happy, but what they really wanted was a brand-new Taylor Swift album! Luckily for them, they wouldn't have to wait much longer.

☆ ☆ CHAPTER 12 ☆ ☆

Fearless

Taylor has a problem—or maybe it isn't a problem so much as a need. "I absolutely can't stop writing songs," she admitted to *Rolling Stone*. "It's funny because sometimes you'll hear artists talking about how they have to hurry up and write this next record and it's like, I can't stop writing. I can't turn it off. I go through situations and I go through experiences and I go through life and I need to write it. I need to write it down. It's like breathing. It's kind of interesting because whenever I've gone in to record albums, I mean, we're going through like a hundred songs and trying to pick the best one."

Nobody was surprised, then, when Taylor announced back in mid-2008 that she was working on a new album. Her fans were all thrilled—they loved Taylor's debut album and wanted more from the young singer-songwriter. And Taylor was just as enthusiastic. "I am so excited about it," she told the *Modesto Bee*. "There is so much I wanted to put on the first album, I can't even wait. I am so excited about giving these people who have done so much for me and have had the (first) album this entire time something new to latch on to. They've been so supportive of these 12 songs of mine, I want to give them more."

Taylor takes her singing very seriously, and she tries to make each song, each album, and each performance as good as it can possibly be. She was determined that her second all-new album would be even better than her first. She worked with several new partners, including John Rich, of Big & Rich, and fellow singer Colbie Caillat, best known for her hit "Bubbly," to produce something new and fresh but still uniquely Taylor Swift. With Colbie, she wrote the song "Breathe," which Taylor says is about losing a close friendship. "I'm extremely excited about the song I wrote with Colbie. It's so my favorite thing on the record already . . . It's got a very cool vibe about it. It's hard to put my finger on it—it's a moment," Taylor told the *Kalamazoo Gazette*.

Taylor decided to stick to subject matters she knew firsthand for her new songs—that meant boys, crushes, and friendships. One thing Taylor knew she wouldn't want to write about is being famous. "I'm not going to write songs about what it's like being on the road. I know 99 percent of my fans can't relate to that. I will write songs about things I can relate to and the people buying my album can relate to," Taylor told the *Miami Herald*. Taylor wanted to make sure that she wrote songs her fans would want to listen to over and over again. As she explained to the *Modesto Bee,* "I think to succeed over a long period of time, you have to not reflect back on the success you have so far. For the second album, I am going to make it like the first album. I am going to put out eight songs I think can be singles, not just three or four. Record companies want you to only put three or four great songs on an album, with the rest filler, so [as] not to waste a single. But I want to put out great songs for people. As long as I am making people as happy as they are making me, I will feel like I've accomplished something."

Taylor's second full album, *Fearless*, was released

in the United States on November 11, 2008. The album debuted at number 1 on the Billboard 200 Album Chart. It sold almost six hundred thousand copies, the highest debut of any country artist in 2008. That impressive sales figure was also the largest opening US sales week in 2008 by a female artist in any genre of music, and the fourth biggest overall behind Lil Wayne, AC/DC, and Coldplay.

More than one hundred and twenty thousand of Swift's sales that opening week were digital sales. That meant *Fearless* had the most impressive initial online sales of any country album in history! It was the fourth biggest week for a digital album since Nielsen SoundScan started tracking digital sales in 2004. By its eighth week out, *Fearless* had sold almost three hundred and forty thousand downloads, making it the best-selling country album in digital history! And the album in second place? Taylor's debut album, *Taylor Swift*, which had almost two hundred and forty thousand downloads as of mid-April, 2009.

The songs from the album did incredibly well individually as well. In its debut week, seven of the songs from *Fearless* were on the Billboard Hot 100, which meant Taylor had tied Miley Cyrus's alter-ego, Hannah Montana, for the most Top 100 songs by a female artist in a single week. The single "Love Story" was released on September 12, 2008, along with a music video based on Shakespeare's tragic love story *Romeo and Juliet*, and reached number 2 on the iTunes Store Top Downloaded Songs and number 4 on the Billboard Hot 100. A few months later, "Love Story" started being played on pop radio stations as well as country stations, and became the first country crossover recording to hit number 1 on the Nielsen BDS CHR/Top 40 chart in the list's sixteen-year history. It also hit number 1 on the Mediabase Top 40 chart. The single "White Horse" was released on December 8 and reached number 13 on the Billboard Hot 100, giving Taylor her sixth Top 20 debut of 2008 and earning her the record for most Top 20 debut songs from an artist in one calendar year in the history of the Billboard Hot 100! The music video for "White Horse" premiered on CMT on February 7, 2009. The song claimed number 2 on Billboard's Hot Country Songs list in

April, and number 1 on the USA Today/Country Aircheck chart that same week. One of the album's tracks, "Change," was selected as part of a soundtrack supporting Team USA's efforts in the 2008 Summer Olympics. The song was also featured as part of the soundtrack of NBC's broadcast package of the Olympics. Eleven of *Fearless*'s thirteen tracks ultimately made it onto the Hot 100, which makes for one hot album indeed!

By the end of the year, the numbers were in, and Nielsen SoundScan showed that Taylor was a clear winner. *Fearless* had finished as the top country record of the year and the third best-selling album of the year period, with over two million sales! And *Taylor Swift* was right behind it at number 6 with roughly one-and-a-half million! Together, they made Taylor the biggest selling artist in America! She was the first artist in Nielsen SoundScan's history to have two different albums in the year-end Top 10 chart. *Fearless* had topped the Billboard 200 for a total of eleven weeks, more than any album since 2000. It was the first album put out by a female in country music history to sit at number 1 on the Billboard

200 for eight full weeks. By the middle of January 2009, Taylor had become the first country artist to hit two million paid downloads on three different songs. And by the start of February, "Love Song" had more paid downloads than any country song in history, and became the first country song to top the mainstream Top 40 chart as well. Not that Taylor was surprised by the album's cross-genre appeal. "I never think of genre or demographics, but more about melodies," she told the *Evansville Courier & Press*. "And just because there are people who say I'm not country enough when I'm writing my songs, I do not 'country them up.'"

In April, Taylor received further proof of *Fearless*'s success. The 44th Annual Academy of Country Music Awards was held on April 5, 2009, in Las Vegas, and *Fearless* was up for Album of the Year! Taylor started the evening in a gorgeous, crimson, one-shouldered Angel Sanchez dress, her hair pulled back in a loose braid to show off both her bare neck and her Neil Lane teardrop earrings. Of course, she was performing as well—magician David Copperfield literally conjured her onto the stage,

117

and then she sang her single "You're Not Sorry" for the rapt audience. For the performance, she changed into a black chiffon dress heavily embellished with gold sequins, and black, calf-length studded boots. She styled her hair in ringlets and completed the look with thick, black eyeliner, black mascara, and fuchsia lip balm. And if Taylor thought the night couldn't get any better, she was wrong—*Fearless* wound up winning Album of the Year! But Taylor was in for another surprise as well. At the end of the evening, she was given a second award, the ACM Crystal Milestone Award for Outstanding Achievement in Country Music, specifically for helping to bring so many young fans to country music. Taylor was thrilled, of course. "The fact that you can write songs in your bedroom about your feelings and boys, and can win album of the year at the ACMs—I just didn't think that was possible," she said as she accepted the award for *Fearless*. What a night!

"Ok," Taylor blogged a few days later. "The ACM's were last week. WOW. What a night! I can't believe I got to accept 2 awards, and winning

Album of the Year absolutely blew me away. I won two awards because I was the artist and the co-producer on *Fearless*. I write songs in my bedroom, and have so much fun doing this, it doesn't really feel like work. The fact that you can win Album of the Year for that was just unbelievable to me. And after I performed, Reba [McEntire] surprised me by giving me the Crystal Milestone award for selling more records than anyone else this year. I can't thank you guys enough for making the album the success story that it has been this year. That's all you. Thank you. Thank you. Thank you. THANK YOU."

So how did Taylor put together such an amazing album? The same way she does everything else, apparently—she just did it her own way! "I don't like to sit down and have a game plan for how an album's going to turn out," she confessed to *Channel Guide Magazine*. "I just like to put the best songs that I've written on an album, and put as many songs on it as I can possibly put it, and release as many songs as I can possibly release, and hope for the best. That's what we did for the first album and hopefully we get similar results with the second album. I'm really excited about it. I coproduced this album, as well as wrote every song on it, so it'll be really fun."

The album is definitely fun, and definitely a colossal success. All because Taylor does things her way, earnestly and honestly, and with a lot of hard work and enthusiasm. Is there any wonder she's fearless?

CHAPTER 13

Investigating the Scene

These days, most musicians can't get away with just sitting, playing their instrument, and singing for an audience. It's a performance, and some musicians take that aspect of it a bit further than others. Taylor loves performing—she loves dressing up, loves elaborate sets, and loves making a big production out of it. That's reflected not only in her music videos but in her live performances as well, where she's incorporated multiple costume changes and some innovative set designs to create a more engaging experience for all the fans who come to her shows.

Is it any wonder, then, that true acting is only a short hop away? And given that she's so used to working in front of cameras already, that Taylor might decide to try her hand at television?

Taylor's been on television before, of course. In

2008, she made her acting debut in Brad Paisley's music video "Online." Of course, she and Kellie Pickler were actually touring with him at the time, so playing the backup singers during the portions of the video where he performed onstage wasn't much of a stretch, though it did get more interesting when Jason Alexander was pretending to be Paisley! It was also a fun way for Taylor to experience being on camera in someone else's video for a change.

That same year, she filmed a documentary for MTV entitled *MTV's Once Upon a Prom*, where MTV followed her to a senior prom at Hillcrest High in Tuscaloosa, Alabama. Taylor had missed her own senior prom due to scheduling conflicts—instead, during the one-hour special, she selected a date from a group of dateless teen boys, chose a dress, and did her best to have the perfect prom experience. Apparently it worked, too—Taylor later told *People*, "It was literally one of the best nights of my life!" She wound up attending with Whit Wright, who she picked from about fifty applicants. "This guy was so down to earth and all-American," she said. "He was unbelievably sweet." Taylor wore a pale pink Sue Wong dress to match Wright's pink vest and tie (worn to honor a friend's mother who is battling breast cancer) and they double-dated with Taylor's best friend, Abigail, and Wright's best friend, Wayne. How did the date go? "I don't kiss on the first date!" Taylor insisted, but told *People* she'd be happy to see him again. "He was the best prom date ever!"

A few months later, Taylor filmed another documentary, this time for CMT. It was an episode of *CMT Crossroads*, a show which features a pairing between a country singer or band and a rock singer or band, and her episode featured Taylor and her band performing with legendary rock band Def Leppard. This was a real treat for Taylor because she'd grown up listening to their music. "My mom listened to Def Leppard when she was pregnant with me," she revealed to *Channel Guide Magazine*. "It's pretty much ingrained into my genetics that I am to love Def Leppard, so it's really cool to get to do this with them." Taylor had actually suggested the idea the summer before, when she'd been on tour with Tim McGraw and Faith Hill. Their tour manager,

Robert Allen, was Def Leppard drummer Rick Allen's brother, and, when Taylor found that out, she asked Robert to put her in touch with the rock band. He did, and Taylor told Rick about *Crossroads*. A few months later, her record label called to tell her that Def Leppard had contacted them and they were interested in doing the show with her.

It wound up being an amazing experience. "There was this moment where Rick Allen was testing his drum kit and they set up their instruments and everything first," she told *Rolling Stone*, "and we were all sitting around watching, my band, my mom and I. You know the signature drum hit for 'Pour Some Sugar On Me' the first time you hear it. It's absolutely unmistakable. The first time he hit it, my band and I just erupted and were just looking at each other like, 'This is not happening, you've got to be kidding me.'" But it did happen, and both bands had a great time performing together. And it shows! The episode premiered on November 7, 2008, and drew more than 4.5 million viewers over its four airings.

Next Taylor collaborated with the Jonas Brothers

in their 3-D concert film, *Jonas Brothers: The 3D Concert Experience*. The film showed both a live concert performance and backstage footage, and Taylor performed her song "Should've Said No" with the trio. The concert film brought in $12.7 million on its opening weekend.

On January 10, 2009, Taylor added another credit to her résumé. She made her first musical guest appearance on *Saturday Night Live*, becoming the youngest country singer to guest star on the show in its thirty-three-year run. The episode got the highest adult eighteen-to-forty-nine rating and overall viewer total *SNL* had seen since the November election the year before.

Those were all Taylor playing herself, however. Next she wanted to try something different. She wanted to become someone else, just like any other actor. And she knew exactly which show she wanted to be on!

Taylor made her primetime television acting debut on CBS's *CSI: Crime Scene Investigation* on March 5, 2009. Over twenty million viewers tuned in to watch the episode, titled "Turn, Turn, Turn." "It was an indescribable feeling," she told the *Evansville Courier*. "On my bus, I have every [*CSI*] DVD, so meeting the people and actually being with them was very exciting. I was a very different person in that role. I got killed and that was really weird." It's unusual to see Taylor flustered about anything, but she admitted to *CBS News* beforehand that "I'm so excited, because I'm going to freak out and probably cry when I meet all my favorite characters. I'm so excited [for it], and I can't wait."

Why is Taylor such a big *CSI* fan? "With *CSI: Las Vegas*, it kind of pairs up all of the things that I'm obsessed with, other than music," she explained to *CBS News*. "When I see really cool editing and really cool effects done, I admire it, and I like to go back and watch it again." The stories intrigue her as well. "I also love the whole crime-scene aspect of it, of figuring things out and analyzing." Sounds like having her on the show was a perfect fit!

That doesn't mean it was easy, however! As Taylor told *Entertainment Tonight*, "I've watched the show for so long, but in the beginning when you see the dead bodies you don't realize that those are people that are sitting really still and holding their breath and having their eyes in one direction, because they're so good at it." And this time, it was Taylor's turn to play the stiff! In Taylor's episode, her character, Haley Jones, is a teenage girl whose family runs a seedy Vegas motel plagued with murders and other unfortunate incidents. Over the course of a year, Haley goes through a series of changes that have tragic consequences. Nick Stokes (*CSI* stalwart George Eads) is the one called in to investigate because he's met Haley several times over the course of that year, due to other cases at the same motel. Most of the story was told through flashbacks, as Nick remembered their previous encounters—and those incidents wound up providing evidence to explain what had happened to Haley, and why.

Since then, Taylor has made a cameo appearance in Kellie Pickler's music video "Best Days of Your Life" and appeared in *Hannah Montana: The Movie* as "woman singing in the bar." The film was released on April 10, 2009, in the US and grossed $17.4 million in its opening day and $32 million over its opening weekend. By mid-May 2009, it had grossed over $84 million worldwide. Only two months before the film's debut, Taylor had shared a different stage with her pal Miley Cyrus, as the two performed Taylor's song "Fifteen" together at the fifty-first Grammy Awards on February 8, 2009. Taylor wore a stunning, sleeveless black Kaufman Franco gown for the occasion, with Rene Caovilla heels and Lorraine Schwartz jewels—though she changed to something a little more casual before climbing up on a stool with her guitar for the song!

Will Taylor decide to do more acting in the future? "Maybe," she told the *Evansville Courier*. But it's never going to be her first choice: "I love acting, but I can live without acting. I can't live without music." Fortunately, with her penchant for impressive concert performances and clever music videos, Taylor can probably continue to get the best of both worlds.

☆☆ CHAPTER 14 ☆☆
A Tour of Her Own

One thing Taylor and her fans had always hoped for was a Taylor Swift tour. Taylor had toured with some of the biggest names in country music, so she was sure she could put on an amazing show as a headliner. And it was an important milestone in any musician's career. As she told the *St. Petersburg Times* in early 2007, "Well, in five years, I will be 22 going on 23. I see myself living in a little house, an old house that's really pretty and decorated really cute. But I won't see it a lot because I want to stay on the road and I want to be headlining. That's my dream, to be on a headlining tour, because that means you've got longevity and you've got thousands of people that are willing to come out and see you every night." Not surprisingly, it didn't take Taylor five years to achieve that dream!

Taylor was determined to do things properly,

however. "I'm very fascinated with the music industry, the touring industry and the business end of things," she told *Rolling Stone*, "so I've paid attention to other careers, the timing and decisions that were made in other careers. I've seen it happen where you have a successful first record, and they throw you out as a headliner way too early and it doesn't work. You never want to have to go backwards. I don't have an ego issue. I'm cool being an opening act. I'd rather be an opening act longer than I should, than headline too early." So, was Taylor finally ready for that next big step? She thought so! "So, now we're headlining," she continued. "I'm starting to headline this summer and I'm really excited about that because I feel like I waited so long, that I want it so bad, and I can't wait. I'm going to throw everything I have into this headlining tour. I feel like we're in a place where I can really put together a great tour."

In January 2009, Taylor announced her first headlining tour. The tour would center on her second album, *Fearless*, and would visit fifty-two cities in thirty-eight different states and provinces in the United States and Canada over the span of six months. Friend and fellow singer Kellie Pickler signed on to be one of the opening acts. "I'm so excited that Kellie's coming out to open up," Taylor wrote on her blog. "She's been one of my best friends since we toured together a few years ago, and it's gonna be hilarious to be on the road with her again. I can't wait to go over to her bus and hang out with her and all of her tiny little animals that she has rapidly acquired. Between the cat, the dog, the snake, and the monkey . . . It's going to be a trip. Or a zoo. Or both. I love her and I'm so lucky she's coming out with me."

Taylor had another opening act lined up as well. "There's this new group called Gloriana that's coming out with us," she explained on her blog. "They're AMAZING and I love their new single 'Wild at Heart.' I heard it and immediately knew I wanted them on this tour. Check them out, I think you'll agree. Everyone in Nashville is buzzing about them and now I get to have them out with ME this summer. Yessssss."

In addition to her opening acts, Taylor had her own band that accompanied her for all her songs.

The band's lineup had changed slightly, however. "There are a bunch of new people you're going to see with us this year on that stage," she reported on her blog. "First of all, we have six new dancers who can point their toes and twirl and stuff with the best of them. On the band side, we've added another backup singer and her name is Liz. And she's precious and amazing. You might have seen her perform with us on Leno. That was her first TV gig with us. Another change I wanted to give you guys the heads up on: Unfortunately, you won't see Ben playing banjo with us anymore. :(We're gonna miss him so much, but he's got dreams and wanted to pursue them. We're all so close to him, we'll never stop seeing him around. All the best. :) But there's good news . . . We've got the insanely talented Mike Meadows playing banjo/mandolin/guitar/keys/cello now (told you he was ridiculous. Count that list of instruments. For those of you who would rather not do unnecessary math on a weekend, that's five instruments.) Mike is hilarious and fits right in with us. He and Liz are part of the family now and I can't wait for you to see what they can do. They've joined

'The Agency' (my band has referred to themselves as The Agency since they got to dress up in suits and sunglasses and ransack a house in the 'Picture to Burn' video. The scene of them walking across the yard in slow motion only encouraged this.) So now it's Grant, Paul, Amos, Al, Caitlin, Liz, and Mike. I love it."

Taylor had big plans for her tour, of course. As she told *Rolling Stone*, "For my concerts, I really don't want people to be seeing the same thing for more than two songs in a row. For my headlining shows, when I actually am allowed to have my own stage and my own production, I've already drawn up the stage plan and what I want it to look like. It's going to look nothing like the headlining tours that I've supported in the past two years. I feel like there's drama that I've always been attracted to—sort of a theatrical type, dramatic performance that I feel is sometimes missing when you see shows these days. I never want people to think that they're just seeing a show where I'm playing song, after song, after song. When I play a song, I want people to feel like they're experiencing exactly what I went through when I

133

wrote the song as I'm singing it for them. There are set ups that I really want to create. There are visuals that I'm really excited about, and I can't wait for you to come out and see a show."

Some of the elements include visuals and background images—Taylor is fascinated by video editing, and loves the idea of using projected images to create environments for her songs. There are also several costume changes, because she enjoys dressing appropriately for each number. There are elaborate sets, including a fairy-tale castle. And Taylor planned to play the piano as well as five different guitars— though she's not as skilled on the piano as she is on the guitar, Taylor does play it well enough to perform her songs in concert.

Before heading out on tour, there were a few other projects on Taylor's plate that she had to take care of first. And though they weren't as big as a headline tour, they were still important to her—and to her fans.

On March 20, 2009, for example, Taylor got to play another venue she'd heard a lot about but never dreamed she'd get to perform: the Houston Rodeo!

She wrote in her blog, "I'm wiped out. I've been in the studio all day (I know, I know. We JUST put out a new album. I think I have a problem, I cannot stop writing songs.) It's so much fun knowing that you can take your time, because you have like a year and a half to make something you're really proud of. I love recording a few songs, waiting a few months, recording a few more. Instead of devoting a few weeks to 'record the album' and then it's just done. I like dragging it out, that way you can be meticulous about every detail. Daydream about different ways to put the songs together, and then take them apart. I'm pretty obsessed with the whole process. So needless to say, it was good to be back in the studio with my redheaded producer who I missed terribly.

"Tomorrow I play the Houston Rodeo for the first time in my life. I've heard about it since I was born because my mom's from Houston. They're telling me really crazy things about the ticket sales so far, and I'm kind of in shock about how many of your beautiful faces I'm going to be seeing tomorrow. I'm really excited about it, and I'd love to see you there!

"When we get back from Texas, I go straight into tour rehearsals for the Fearless tour. (!!!!) I can't believe this is actually, really . . . happening. They've set my stage up in this giant, massive warehouse and apparently it's really something. Considering that the stage was originally inspired from a drawing I made a few years ago, I'll be the most excited person in the room when we go over and see it for the first time. Then we start the hard part: Putting the show together.

"Again, I know I say thank you every 4 seconds, but, guys, thanks for all of this. Wish me luck. See you in Houston."

The Houston Rodeo concert was a smashing success. Over seventy-two thousand people turned out to hear Taylor perform, making that night the eighth most-attended in the rodeo's history! And Taylor didn't send people away disappointed—the *Houston Chronicle* reported afterward, "She was alternately sassy and demure, working the stage like a seasoned pro. And her voice has gotten stronger and more commanding." It was an excellent night for Taylor, and an excellent prediction of good things to come on her tour.

Taylor's North American Fearless Tour 2009 launched on April 23 in Evansville, Indiana. But tickets for the May 22 performance at Los Angeles's Staples Center actually went on sale first, on February 6—and sold out in two minutes! Tickets for several dates and venues, including New York City's famed Madison Square Garden, went on sale the following week and also sold out quickly.

Two weeks before the first show, Taylor wrote on her blog: "I know that I use the word 'excited' in my blogs more than any other word in the English language, but I have to say . . . I'm really excited right now. It's really hitting me that I get to go on my first headlining tour. With a big stage. And I'm not opening up for people anymore. And I get to pick what we eat in catering! (I recommended an all cupcake menu, but apparently that doesn't meet everyone's dietary needs for survival. The idea was vetoed. You can't win them all I guess). I get to pick out how the backstage area is decorated. And I love decorations. And backstage areas. There are so many different decisions to be made regarding video content and lighting and changes. So basically . . . I'm excited."

According to the *Evansville Courier & Press*, Taylor hit the ground running and wowed the crowd right from the start of the first performance. "After a two hour show at Roberts Stadium backed with a solid band, dancers, a morphing stage set and special effects," they reported, "it's easy to understand why Taylor Swift's music has become a radio sensation." After she hit St. Louis on April 25, the website STLtoday.com stated that "Swift handled herself well, coming off surprisingly assured and earnest during the near two-hour concert." On April 30, Taylor was in Charleston, South Carolina, where, the next day, the *Post & Courier* commented, "If Thursday's ambitious production is any indication of how Swift plans to make her mark in the entertainment world, then at the ripe old age of 19 it appears that we can expect some truly huge things from this star in the future."

The last tour stop on Taylor's tour is Minneapolis/ St. Paul, on October 10. Taylor is also scheduled to perform with Keith Urban ten times over the course of the year, somehow fitting those appearances in between her own tour dates. It's certainly going to be a busy year for her!

☆☆ CHAPTER 15 ☆☆
Future Plans

Taylor has had an exhausting ride since she signed her record deal with Big Machine Records back in 2005. She's been on multiple tours, released two albums, had a bunch of hit singles, watched her albums go double- and triple-platinum, won several awards, and made country music history. That's not too shabby—especially since that was all before she even turned twenty years old! For a lot of people, now would be the perfect time for a vacation, but not for Taylor.

As things calm down, Taylor would like to return to her roots and do some songwriting for other artists. One time, when Taylor's close friend Kellie Pickler got some bad news out on the road during the girls' tour with Brad Paisley, Taylor helped her deal with it. "Kellie came on my bus this summer and was all upset about her ex-boyfriend. She was like, 'I just want to be over this!' And she gets up on stage now and tells everyone all about it. And I'm like, 'Okay, if you want to tell everyone your personal stuff, but there's no better way to get over something than to write it all down.' So we went into the back bedroom of my tour bus and wrote this awesome song. It's about how, for the rest of his life, he's going to regret cheating on her. And she's said to me since then, 'You know what, I didn't think there was anything I could do to really get past that. But writing that song gave me complete closure,'" Taylor told theboot.com. Taylor loved writing a song from someone else's point of view. As she explained to CMT.com, ". . . it was so cool jumping into someone else's feelings for a minute and writing from their perspective. It was like I was writing my very first song. Exhilarating."

One thing Taylor has been doing all along—and plans to continue to do in the future— is give back to her community. Taylor has been known to give her personal phone number out to fans she meets who are going through a hard time and she spends what little free time she has answering fan mail, but that's not enough for her. As a huge MySpace fan, Taylor loves connecting with people online, but she also knows that the Internet can be a very dangerous place for kids. So she teamed up with Phil Bredesen, the governor of Tennessee, for a statewide program called "Delete Online Predators." The goal of the program is to educate middle-school students and their parents about safe Internet use. Taylor's goal is for all students to sign the NetSmartz "Internet Safety Pledge," a promise to protect themselves online developed by the National Center for Missing and Exploited Children. "Chatting with friends and surfing the Internet is cool. But it's important to stay safe. Be smart about keeping your identity private online," Taylor told *That's Country*. The campaign includes school visits, distribution of brochures with tips for online safety, distribution of NetSmartz Safety Pledge brochures with a special message from Taylor, and wristband giveaways.

Taylor also performed in the 2008 Sprint Speed and Sound Concert to benefit the Victory Junction Gang Camp, a children's charity that helps kids with terminal diseases. "They have camps all over the country for kids who are sick. It's one week . . . they forget they're sick and just have a blast and hang out with other people who they can relate to. They look forward to it, and I love that cause," Taylor explained to people.com. She even made a very special donation to the charity on January 10, 2008—her birthday present from her label, a pink Chevy pickup truck. "My label was so awesome to give me this amazing truck for my birthday. The moment I saw it, in all its pink glory, I knew that the kids at the Victory Junction Gang Camp would love it," Taylor explained to frontstretch.com. Causes that affect children are dear to Taylor and you can be sure she'll be involved in many more of them in the future.

Taylor's career is on fire, she's got family and friends who love her, and she's working toward accomplishing many more of the goals she's set for herself, but is there anything she'd like to do that she's going to miss out on? Most of Taylor's friends are either in college now or getting ready to go, while Taylor is putting aside thoughts of higher education for a while. "Of course, you're always going to wonder about the road not taken, the dorm not taken, and the sorority not taken. But if I wasn't doing this, I would've missed out on the best moments I've ever known and the most wonderful life that I still can't believe I get to live. I'm still friends with the same people I was friends with in high school, and I feel like I haven't changed as a person," Taylor explained to CMT.com.

She does plan to continue her education when time permits, as she told the *St. Petersburg Times*. "I would love to take a class every once in a while, but I really cannot walk away from this for four years. Four years is a long time. People will fill your spot." Instead, Taylor has been getting a different kind of education than her peers by working in the business that she loves. "I think anyone, when they come across something that fascinates them more than anything they've ever seen—and that's what music does for me—I think when each person finds that in their life, that's when they become driven," Taylor explained to the *Philadelphia Inquirer*. "That's when they grow up. I was just kind of a fluke in that I found mine at age 10. I was like: I

145

found this. There's no way I can let it go."

For now, Taylor has to content herself with living the college life vicariously. Best bud Abigail won a swimming scholarship to the University of Kansas, and keeps Taylor updated on life on a major college campus. On April 27, 2009, Taylor even took time out of her concert tour schedule to stop by for a visit! That wound up being a little less low-key than she'd probably planned, though. Taylor decided to sit in on a college class, and accompanied Abigail to her journalism lecture. But even in a large lecture hall, it's tough for Taylor to go unnoticed—or unrecognized. People began to whisper, and to stare, and soon text messages and twitters were flying. By the end of class, more than fifty students were waiting outside hoping to catch a glimpse of the country superstar. Of course, Taylor being Taylor, she was happy to meet her fans, and spent some time signing autographs and taking pictures with people before leaving. Oh, and the class? "Media and Society." Seems appropriate!

Taylor certainly hopes she'll have a long and successful career, but she doesn't really want to be compared to anyone. "You know, I'm not really looking to model my career after anyone. I'm looking to do something new. I want to do everything new. I mean country music will always be country music . . . but the audiences can be changed and expanded. I think it would be great if when I'm 90 years old and looking back on life, I can say I did things people didn't expect and was successful," Taylor told GACtv.com. Don't worry, Taylor—you've already changed country music for the better!

For now, Taylor is concentrating on her Fearless concert tour. No doubt there will be another album in the near future—given how many songs she writes, she'll probably have enough material before the tour ends! She's also going to be performing at several more awards shows, starting with the Country Music Television Awards on June 16, along with Toby Keith, Brad Paisley, Rascal Flatts, and others. And in 2009, Taylor became the National Hockey League's newest celebrity spokesperson. She appears in commercials for her favorite team, the Nashville Predators, and was recently seen at an L.A. Kings hockey game with bud Demi Lovato.

The question isn't how Taylor will keep busy.

The question is when she's planning to slow down—if ever! "I would love to make music for the next 30 years," she told *Channel Guide Magazine*. "I don't know if I want to be walking red carpets in 30 years. In 30 years, I'll be 48 and I'll have wrinkles—because we're probably not going to get rid of wrinkles surgically—and I'm probably going to have some gray hairs." That probably won't be a problem for her, though. Odds are, Taylor will still be stunning in her late forties, and will still be making heads turn, on and off the stage. She certainly plans to be writing and singing and to be heavily involved in the industry for a long time to come. "When people look back on my career," she told the *Vanderbilt Hustler*, "I'd love for them to look at what I've done and say 'wow, she wrote songs for herself but she also wrote that hit for someone else, and then someone else.' I'd love for people to look back and say that I never took anything for granted and I appreciated everything that was ever given to me because everything can be taken away if I make one wrong move. I want people to look back and realize that I was really respectful of the music industry and my career—and that I sold millions and millions of albums." She's certainly doing all of that already, and we can't see any reason Taylor won't continue to be a tremendous songwriter and performer and a major influence on country music, music in general, and people everywhere.

☆☆ CHAPTER 16 ☆☆
In Her Spare Time

When Taylor isn't on tour or in the studio, she's just another teenager who loves hanging out with her friends and giggling about boys, eating junk food, and going to the mall. Taylor is not afraid to admit that she's horrible at sports, but loves doing yoga, and she's completely addicted to *Law & Order: SVU, CSI*, and *Grey's Anatomy*. Her lucky number is thirteen, and she is superstitious about it, as she explained to the *Philadelphia Inquirer*. "I was born on Dec. 13, and I turned 13 on Friday the 13th. And from the point where my album was released until it went platinum was exactly 13 months."

The outgoing message on her cell phone even sounds just like any other teenager's. "Hey, it's Taylor. I can't get your call right now but call back like 100 times and I'll get back to you," Scott Borchetta, the head of her record label told GACtv.com. But unlike a lot of teenagers, you won't find Taylor out at wild parties or sneaking into bars. "I'm just really more of a laid-back person. I've never been a party girl," Taylor explained to *Entertainment Weekly*.

Even during her off-hours, Taylor knows that her fans will be watching to see what she does. And that's fine with her, because Taylor isn't like a lot of other stars her age. "When I'm about to make decisions, my point of reference is the 6-year-old girl in the front row of my concert. I think about what she would think if she saw me do what I was considering doing. Then I go back and I think about her mom and what her mom would think if I did that," Taylor told *Entertainment Weekly*. Taylor has never given in to peer pressure to do anything. She's in no hurry to grow up, and, as far as she is concerned, there shouldn't be room in any kid's life for drugs or alcohol.

So what does Taylor do for fun if she's not out all night at parties? Well, Taylor loves driving around in her car, listening to music. She has a Lexus SC 430 hardtop convertible she bought with the money from those first songs she sold professionally. As her friends like to point out, it's the same car the popular girls drive in the hit movie *Mean Girls* starring Lindsay Lohan. The car has gotten its fair share of dings and scrapes, but Taylor doesn't care. "I am monogamous when it comes to my car," she told *Women's Health*.

Taylor also enjoys spending time on Old Hickory Lake with her family. The Swifts still live in the same house they lived in when they first moved to Nashville, and now they have two boats, a 420 Sundancer and a 220 Sundeck, and they spend a lot of sunny days outside boating.

When she's in Los Angeles, Taylor also hangs out with one of her newest buddies, actress and fellow singer Selena Gomez (best known for her role as Alex Russo on the Disney Channel original series *Wizards of Waverly Place*). "I'd say Selena Gomez is definitely my best friend in the business," Taylor told justjaredjr.com. "We talk all the time, almost everyday. She's just such a cool person because she's so real and a lot of times people get to a level where they're famous and people know them, people recognize them and they become . . . less real and Selena's so cool because she's got a great sense of humor, she's a real person. It's really awesome to have gotten to know her and have her in my life."

But Taylor's best friend, Abigail Anderson, is her favorite person to spend most of her time off with. "I have every Sunday off, so I usually spend it with her," Taylor told GACtv.com. The girls like to bake goodies and watch their favorite movie, *Napoleon Dynamite*, over and over. They also like to prank their ex-boyfriends with funny phone calls.

There are some exes, though, that Taylor would rather not see, like Drew Hardwick, Taylor's one-time crush and the inspiration for the song "Teardrops On My Guitar." Since he lives in Hendersonville, she couldn't avoid him forever after her song came out, although she tried. Taylor told *Seventeen* that Drew called her after the single was released, but that she was too nervous to call him back. Eventually he showed up at her house to see her in person. "Kellie Pickler and I were going to a hockey game and this guy pulls up. I didn't have my contacts on and didn't see him right away. He's a little older, a little taller, the guy I wrote that song about 2 1/2 years ago. I hadn't talked to him. I didn't know what to say and here he is walking toward me," Taylor told the *Miami Herald*. But it wasn't nearly as bad as she thought it was going to be to discuss her now-public crush on Drew. "Everything was nice. There was no, like, screaming and 'You're too late!' It was all very cordial," Taylor told Nashville's WKRN Radio. It would have been funny if Drew and Taylor had finally gotten together, but Taylor moved on a long time ago!

As far as boyfriends go, all of the romance in Taylor's life remains in the past. "I'm completely single!" Taylor told theboot.com. "I think that love is something that hits you when you're not looking for it. So I've been actively not looking for it for like two years. I'm always the third wheel on my friends' dates. I have a bunch of best friends who never go more than a month without having a boyfriend. And I think that's kinda rubbed off on me, because I've seen the stuff they've gone through over the past two years. And I'm just like, 'I'm gonna pursue my career instead.'" Taylor has thousands of male fans who would love a chance to get to know the beautiful starlet a little better, but Taylor just isn't interested in finding love at the moment. "I've been in relationships and I thought I was in love. I've never had a love for anything that was enough to make me stop thinking about music. I've been in relationships but there was always something that I needed more. It never filled something that I felt like I was missing. Music is the only thing that could do that. Maybe I'm un-datable right now. I've been going through this independent phase where I haven't been interested in dating at all," she explained to GACtv.com. Taylor's future boyfriends better watch out, though, since she has a habit of singing about her relationships in her songs, and she's not shy about naming names! Hopefully someday Taylor will find a guy who only inspires happy love songs.

For a short while in 2008, Taylor—and her fans—thought that she had finally found that right guy. And he was someone who understood the music business—and the challenge of being young and famous—just as much as she did! That's because Taylor was going out with none other than Joe Jonas, the middle of the three Jonas Brothers. They already knew each other, and had even performed together on *Jonas Brothers: The 3D Concert Experience*. When they started dating that summer, neither one of them would admit it publicly, probably to avoid embarrassing questions. It didn't last, however. Apparently Joe met someone else, specifically actress Camilla Belle, who starred in the Jonas Brothers video "Lovebug." "They've been together since we broke up," Taylor told usmagazine.com. "That's why we broke up—because he met her." And not only did Joe break up with Taylor, he did it over the phone! In less than thirty seconds! Talk about uncool! Of course, Joe claimed things happened a little differently than Taylor had said. "For those who have expressed concern over the '27 second' phone call," he wrote in a letter to his fans, "I called to discuss feelings with the other person. Those feelings were obviously not well received. I did not end the conversation. Someone else did. Phone calls can only last as long as the person on the other end of the line is willing to talk." No matter who hung up on whom, breaking up by phone is still rude! But Taylor got Joe back in typical Taylor Swift fashion. She wrote a song about him, called "Forever &

Always," which is on the *Fearless* album. "[It's] a song about watching somebody completely fade away in a relationship and wondering what you did wrong," she told *People*. But Taylor wasn't done there! She also filmed a MySpace video with a Joe Jonas doll, during which she remarks, "This one even comes with a phone so it can break up with other dolls!" Ouch!

Since Taylor just graduated from high school, and spent her junior and senior years being homeschooled, there's no real chance she'll meet a boy in study hall, either. But she didn't really miss going to a regular high school. "I don't think there's really anything I miss, to be honest. There's a lot less drama when you're touring the country on a major tour. And I've actually been to prom before . . . twice. So I don't want anyone to feel bad for me. It was really great that I got to experience those first two years of high school, and I'll never forget that. I learned a lot. But I feel like I've had the best senior year ever," Taylor told theboot.com.

Taylor kept up with her classes on the road and graduated with the rest of her class in June 2008.

"I do my homeschooling in the mornings usually, then I'll go to meet-and-greets and sound checks. But morning is the only free time I have," Taylor explained to the *Modesto Bee*. One big benefit of homeschooling was that Taylor got the chance to do more creative assignments than she used to. For one of her English papers, she wrote about the country music group Little Big Town. As she told GACtv.com, "I wrote this ten-page paper about them. When it came time to get a gift for them for their platinum album party, I just printed out my report and gave it to them!" Taylor's report was probably the most unique gift that Little Big Town has ever received!

Of course, given her busy schedule, Taylor doesn't always have time for some of the little things. Like decorating, apparently! "My high school diploma was mailed to me," she told justjaredjr.com. "I'm really excited because I didn't test out or get my GED. I actually went through the whole process of home-schooling. It was pretty tough doing it on the road, but I made it a priority and got my diploma in the mail this summer. Very excited about it. I don't know if we have it hung up yet because we haven't really had much time to hang anything up. It's weird, I walk into my room and it's like a time wrap from when I was in eighth grade. I have no new pictures up. It's like all of me in junior high, it's pretty crazy. Hopefully we'll get some time this winter to hang up some new pictures and my diploma and things like that."

Taylor isn't usually big on parties, but she has been known to make an exception or two over the years. She was busy recording her debut album when she turned sixteen and she didn't get a chance to have a "sweet sixteen" party like most girls her age. So, for her eighteenth birthday, Taylor's parents threw her the girliest, pinkest birthday bash that Nashville had ever seen at local hotspot Lot 7. She spent the day registering to vote and getting ready for the party with her closest friends from high school. She chose a hot pink Betsey Johnson dress to wear that night. "It was between this and a black dress, but I knew all my friends would be in black, so I went with the pink. I love pink!" Taylor told *People*. Pink was certainly the color of the night. The whole club was decked out with pink balloons and lights. There was even a photo booth with a pink background! But the biggest pink moment of the night came when Scott Borchetta, president of Taylor's music label, presented her with her birthday gift—a pink Chevrolet pickup truck, which Taylor later donated to her favorite charity. There were over two hundred guests at the party, including fellow country crooners Kellie Pickler, Chuck Wicks, Lady Antebellum, and Big & Rich's John Rich, who led the crowd in singing "Happy Birthday." But Taylor's favorite birthday gift couldn't be wrapped. "What I really wanted for my birthday was a number 1 record, and I got that, too!" Taylor told *People*.

But there are definitely times that Taylor can't pretend she's a normal teenager, like when a fan asked her to sign an autograph on the side of the road after a car accident. "Yeah, somebody hit my car and then asked me to sign a broken piece of my taillight," Taylor told canoe.ca. "Then it was crazy. Five minutes later this other woman saw me on the side of the road and decided that she wanted to get an autograph for her daughter. So she pulled over to get my autograph and then somebody hit her car.

It was quite the experience." Luckily Taylor has an excellent sense of humor and is able to laugh at herself when strange things happen because of her stardom. She knows she'll never be a normal teenager again, but she wouldn't trade in even one second of her amazing career to be back in homeroom hoping to make it big someday. She's managed to stay the same sweet, grounded, hard-working girl she's always been, thanks to good friends and a loving family, and it seems like Taylor might just be one star who can have it all—the great career and a happy, mostly normal home life!

☆☆ CHAPTER 17 ☆☆
That Covers It

Taylor is as beautiful as she is talented, so it's no wonder people want to look at her as well as listen to her! That must be why she keeps showing up in magazines—and on their covers!

In 2008 alone, Taylor was on the covers of *Women's Health*, *Billboard*, *Seventeen*, *US Weekly* (with Lauren Conrad and Hilary Duff), *Redbook* (with fellow country singers Reba McEntire and Martina McBride), and *Cosmo Girl!* And 2009 is proving to be an even busier year!

On March 5, 2009, it was the cover of *Rolling Stone*. "Taylor Swift: Secrets of a Good Girl," it read in large letters. Taylor's head obscured the magazine's famous title, her hair thick and wavy and seeming almost more red than gold, and she was strumming her guitar. Inside, she talked with interviewer Vanessa Grigoriadis about her life, her music, her priorities, her dreams, and her interests. Taylor also kept Grigoriadis on her toes—the interviewer had to go from the set of *CSI* in Los Angeles to Tim McGraw and Faith Hill's nearby mansion to a press junket in New York and then to the Swift family home in Nashville just to keep up! It was well worth it for the story, though, and to get more insight into Taylor's true personality. What did the interviewer find out? "She really is that girl in the tiny little bedroom at home writing songs about the things she hopes and dreams and feels," Grigoriadis revealed.

Later that same month, Taylor graced the cover of *Self* magazine. She stood confidently, wearing a sleeveless V-necked white top and yellow jeans, her hair loose and in ringlets against her shoulders but brushed back on the right to show off her earrings— and the *Self* masthead beside her. Her jeans and the magazine title were the same hue, and both popped against the cover's pink background. "Taylor Swift: On Love, Life, and Listening to Yourself," the cover proclaimed. Inside, she talked about gifts, fans, honesty, and her favorite background music for photo shoots. Why background music? "You need to be in the right energy and mood," she told *Self*, "so I made a playlist I am very, very proud of." And what did that playlist include? "Jesse McCartney, Justin Timberlake—both are absolutely pivotal to the success of a photo shoot. Britney Spears and Lady Gaga, Beyoncé—very, very necessary. It's a pretty good playlist. They are so good that you can listen to them over and over. You can't do a photo shoot without music." Spoken like a true musician!

In April 2009, it was *Allure* magazine. The cover showed Taylor, hair streaming around her, lips a glossy bright red. The tagline read: "Taylor Swift: Love, Heartache, and her Triple-Platinum Life." Inside, she talked about a variety of topics, including her opinion on classic fairy-tale endings: "I have always been fascinated with fairy tales, and the idea that Prince Charming is just one castle away. And you're gonna run across a field and meet each other in the middle, and have an amazing, perfect movie kiss. And it's gonna be happily ever after."

Then Taylor talked to the magazine about writing that perfect breakup song: "For some reason, I could never, ever stop writing songs about heartbreak. Just because as human beings, what we can't have is what we replay in our head over and over again before we go to sleep."

She also talked about how grateful she was for her fans. "I never would have sold any records if my fans hadn't gone out and bought them. It's so incredible to go out and sign autographs for nine hours straight. That's just my favorite thing to do, honestly."

In May 2009, Taylor graced the cover of *Seventeen* magazine a second time. For the cover she wore a sleeveless one-shouldered purple dress with a wildflower necklace, and had her hair loose and super-curly. For the interior shots, however, she got glammed up in flapper-inspired headbands and accessories while she let her curls run wild. Taylor told justjaredjr.com, "Being on the cover of *Seventeen* was something that I'd always dreamed of as a little girl. For the first time last year, I got to be on the cover and I got the subscription mailed to my house and I just . . . (covers her mouth with her hands) I was so excited. To be on the cover again, in such a short amount of time, is such an honor. The shoot was so much fun! I got here and there were all these crazy accessories. Headbands and birds on hair clips, all these insane things."

Inside the magazine, she talked about putting personal emotions in her songs. "Writing songs about people is the only way I know how to do things. I mean, I can't wish I hadn't written a song about someone, because if I hadn't, that song wouldn't exist. I just don't find any joy in writing about things I haven't been through."

She told *Seventeen* about the subjects she likes to write about. "Right now, my favorite thing to write about is love. And breakups. And boys. And feelings. Honesty is a big part of my writing, because when I was younger and fell in love with songs I'd hear, I would always wonder who that song was about. It would have totally broken my heart to know it wasn't about anyone and was just written so it could be on the radio."

Taylor also talked about her friendships, both famous and not. She and her high school buddy Abigail are still best friends, but when she's in Nashville Taylor also spends time hanging out with pal and fellow singer Kellie Pickler. In Los Angeles, her best buds are actress Selena Gomez, singer-actress Miley Cyrus, singer Demi Lovato, and actress Emma Stone.

May also brought Taylor her first overseas cover, as she appeared on *Dolly* magazine in Australia. "Guitar Hero: Taylor Swift: She Rocks Our World" the cover announced, as Taylor posed in a red top sipping from a soda straw, dangly gold feather earrings emerging from her waved hair and a silver heart bracelet visible on her wrist. Inside, Taylor talked to interviewer Emma V during the Australian leg of her tour. The pair chatted about Taylor's favorite song topics, about boys, about what makes Taylor smile ("When I've just figured out the perfect word to go in that gap I was missing [in a song], that's when I'm at my happiest"), about MySpace, about her last big splurge ("I bought a tour bus . . . it has a treadmill out the back, it has a shower, a complete bathroom, wood floors, a huge bed and a chandelier over the bed. It's really fun!"), and even about what she'd pick for her death row meal ("A huge cheeseburger, large fries, and a chocolate milkshake.").

In June, Taylor continued the overseas trend, this time showing up across the pond on the cover of the UK magazine *Sugar*. "We Love Taylor Swift: 'Why I prefer being single'" is written on the cover. Taylor is standing with her hands behind her head, a mysterious half smile on her lips, her hair blowing about her, a black and gray T-shirt on. She looks comfortable and casual and friendly—all things her fans associate with her! Inside, she talks about boyfriends, Britney Spears, being famous, and her life, including how her parents believe she starting singing early—very early! "Mom says she remembers folding clothes as I lay in my crib, just a few months old, and I started softly cooing," Taylor recounts. "She called my dad in and they were convinced that I was singing to them." Talk about a born musician!

One thing's for sure—Taylor continues to charm interviewers and photographers alike. Most of the people who meet her during these cover shoots talk afterward about how genuinely nice the young star is, and how lovely she is, body and soul. With all that charm and beauty, it's a sure bet Taylor will be gracing covers for years to come!

☆☆ CHAPTER 18 ☆☆
Stylin' Country Girl

One of the coolest things about Taylor is her unique style. If you want to make Taylor's style your own, start with a good pair of cowboy boots. Taylor's favorite pair is made of sky blue leather and they add three inches to her height! They have red and pink detailing and a big heart on the front of each, with "Taylor" written on the right foot and "Swift" on the left. Taylor's boot collection is huge! She wears them with every type of outfit, from fancy dresses to blue jeans. "When you pair a dress with cowboy boots, it's kind of a cool irony to the outfit," Taylor told the *Houston Chronicle*.

Taylor loves dresses. Her favorites are sundresses in summer and tights or leggings with cozy sweaterdresses in winter. She loves fabrics that are comfortable and easy to move in. One thing you won't find her wearing is anything too sexy. In

Taylor's opinion, it's best to leave some things to the imagination!

Of course, Taylor's style has grown over the years. "I've learned a lot," she told *Teen Vogue* when they asked about her glamorous red carpet outfits. "I go to all these photo shoots, and each time I figure out something new about myself and what I want to wear. For a big night, I like Marchesa or Badgley Mischka—and I love Oscar de la Renta. I've never gotten to wear one of his dresses; if I ever did, I would probably faint. And I am obsessed with high heels."

When it comes to accessorizing, Taylor likes to wear big, sparkly earrings, delicate silver chains, multiple bracelets, and headbands. She's never without her leather bracelet with the words "Love Love Love" embossed on it. Taylor keeps most of her makeup very fresh and light, but she loves to experiment with her eyes. She is especially fond of shimmery green, blue, pink, and purple eye shadows and fun eyeliners. As for her beautiful blond hair, "It's been really curly and fro'd out since I was little. I used to fight it. I used to try to straighten it, which turned out horrific. But then I just decided a couple of years ago that I wanted to wear my hair the way that it is. When I'm going on TV, of course, you have the glam squad. They make it look a lot better," Taylor told the *St. Petersburg Times*. For loose curls like Taylor's, try using hot rollers or a curling iron.

For special occasions or performances and appearances, Taylor turns to her personal stylist for help. Sandy Spika has been helping Taylor get stage-worthy for a few years and she always makes Taylor look and feel beautiful. For concerts, Sandy chooses girly sundresses and cowboy boots with fun details. But for awards shows, Sandy goes all out. "I like really long, one-of-a-kind dresses, dramatic massive dresses that take a lot of effort to walk in," Taylor told the *Houston Chronicle*. Sandy hasn't disappointed her client yet, often designing one-of-a-kind originals for Taylor. Taylor also wears lots of Sandy's designs in her music videos.

Taylor is still into comfortable, casual clothing as well, though. And that includes jeans. It had better, seeing as how she's the face of the L.e.i. denim clothing line! That isn't all she's doing with L.e.i., however.

Recently she teamed up with the teen favorite brand to create a new line of sundresses exclusively for sale at Wal-Mart. "I love dresses," Taylor told *People*. "And I have always had this dream to make an affordable sundress line." Affordable is something Taylor's very concerned about. "Everyone's suffering because of the current state of the economy," she pointed out to *For Us* magazine, "so I try to be as conscious of that as possible when I make decisions." That includes offering reasonably priced tickets to her concerts—and producing a sundress line that will retail for around fourteen dollars per dress! "I was totally adamant that I wanted [the dresses] to be affordable," she explained to *People*. "With my headlining tour, we are offering $20 tickets everywhere we go and I wanted to approach the sundress line in the same way."

But did Taylor design the dresses herself? Well, she certainly helped, but the modest singer isn't about to claim all the credit. "I don't look at it like I'm branching out as a designer," she told *New York Magazine*. "It's not the Taylor Swift designer line or whatever. I like people who have worked their entire lives to become designers. I think that they have their place as designers and I have my place as a musician, and I'm going to pretty much stick to that." The lightweight jersey dresses are very cute, however, with their bright colors and attractive prints, and they're exactly the sort of thing Taylor would buy herself. No doubt a lot of her fans will feel the same way!

Taylor's style epitomizes the all-American girl-next-door, and she'll probably never give up that wholesome, fun image for a racier one. It's just not who she is, and she doesn't ever want to be anyone but herself!

☆☆ CHAPTER 19 ☆☆
Swift Details

So you think you're Taylor's biggest fan? Well, here are the fun facts that every Taylor Swift fan should know by heart!

Full name: Taylor Alison Swift

Date of birth: December 13, 1989

Hometown: Wyomissing, Pennsylvania

Height: 5'11"

Hair color: naturally blond and curly

Siblings: younger brother, Austin

Parents: Scott and Andrea Swift

Star sign: Sagittarius

Hobbies: playing guitar, songwriting, driving around listening to music, baking, painting

Best friend: Abigail Lauren Anderson

Instruments: guitar—a Taylor Grand Auditorium acoustic guitar made of koa wood

Biggest musical influences: LeAnn Rimes, Patsy Cline, and her grandmother

Lucky charm: a leather bracelet that says "Love Love Love"

Favorite stores: BCBG, Forever 21, Bebe, and Target and Wal-Mart because "I find the coolest things that you would never expect."

Favorite clothing: dresses and cowboy boots

Favorite Tim McGraw song: "Can't Tell Me Nothin'"

Favorite ice cream: chocolate caramel or vanilla with cookie dough

Pets: a cat named Indi and two Dobermans

Favorite TV show: *Law & Order, CSI,* and *Grey's Anatomy*

Favorite season: summer

Favorite color: pink

Favorite makeup: MAC studio tech, NW20, and nude lip-liner

Favorite designer: Oscar de la Renta. "I've never gotten to wear one of his dresses; if I ever did, I would probably faint."

Favorite sport to watch: hockey

Favorite sports team: the Nashville Predators and the Tennessee Titans

Favorite movie: *Love Actually*

Favorite ringtones: "It's Over" by Jesse McCartney, "You're So Vain" by Carly Simon, and "Low" by Kelly Clarkson

Lucky number: thirteen

Favorite lyrics: "Something written by one of my favorite radio guys, who is also a songwriter: 'If there was no change, there would be no butterflies.' He once sent me a thank-you note and quoted that at the bottom, writing, 'I'm sure everyone is telling you Don't change. But I think the right thing to say is to always embrace change gracefully.' That's a beautiful line."

Celebrity crush: Chace Crawford from *Gossip Girl*

Funniest country & western song title: "She Thinks My Tractor's Sexy"

Weirdest thing in her fridge: apple butter from Cracker Barrel

Who she'd like to be stuck in an elevator with: Ellen DeGeneres. "That situation would panic a lot of people, but she'd be like, 'Hey, whatever!' and make a joke. Then we'd laugh and dance."

How many texts she sends on an average day: Ten. "It's funny, I thought the contact list in my phone would grow if I was in the music industry. But I had more people in my phone book when I was in high school!"

Best Mom advice: "'Don't ever call a guy first. The thing they want the most is whatever they can't have.' It sounds really juvenile, but it works."

Secret talent: grammar

If she wasn't a musician, she'd like to be: a criminal investigator, an advertising executive, or a video editor

☆☆ CHAPTER 20 ☆☆
Which Taylor Are You?

Taylor certainly keeps busy! She's so busy, sometimes it seems like there must be more than one Taylor Swift! Especially since she does so many different things—and does them all so well! There's the down-home Taylor, the country-western girl who loves the outdoors and the open air. There's the glamorous Taylor, who loves dressing up, doing photo shoots, and appearing at awards shows and other events. There's the musician Taylor, who loves writing and performing songs. And then there's the teenage girl Taylor, who loves posting on her MySpace page, going on dates, shopping, and just hanging out with friends. So which Taylor are you most like? Let's find out!

1) It's Saturday morning, the start of the weekend, and you've got the day to yourself! You can do anything you want. So what do you do?

  A. Take a walk along the lake, maybe go swimming, and admire the flowers.

  B. Sort through your clothes, looking for just the right outfit, and get all dressed up to go out and stroll downtown.

  C. Sit and write in your journal, working on a song, and then grab your guitar to test it out.

  D. Call your friends and see if they want to get together and do something, like see a movie or go to the mall.

2) The weekend went too fast, and now it's back to Monday again! But the day is finally over and you can relax a bit. So what do you have planned for tonight?

A. Sit out on the dock with your family and enjoy the cool breeze and sunset.

B. Get dolled up and go to a party or movie premiere—or both?

C. Hit up karaoke night at the local club.

D. Do your homework, text with your friends, and post silly videos on YouTube and MySpace.

3) Your family is trying to decide where to go for summer vacation. Which idea gets your vote?

A. Camping or hiking through the wilderness, far away from cell phones, cars, and cable television.

B. Visiting a big city and seeing all the sights, like the museums, landmarks, and hot spots.

C. Attending several big country music concerts and maybe touring Nashville in between.

185

D. Coordinating something with your best friends, like a beach trip, so you can all go someplace together.

4) Taylor Swift invites you to hang out with her for a day! And she tells you to pick what the two of you get to do! So what is your choice?

    A. Spend the day lying around at the lake, just chilling and talking.

    B. Get all dressed up in your finest duds and go to a celebrity-packed event.

    C. Tour the recording studio, listen to her sing, and maybe even work on a duet!

    D. Paint each other's nails and gossip about boys, including Taylor's famous ex, Joe Jonas!

IF YOU CHOSE . . .

Mostly As—You love nature and just relaxing and enjoying the beauty of the world around you. So does Taylor! Part of her love for country music comes from her appreciation for the great outdoors, and the fact that country music is so honest and direct about life and love and strong emotion.

Mostly Bs—You're all about the glamour! Sometimes Taylor likes to dress up and make appearances on all the hottest red carpets. Plus, her interest in clothes and makeup is reflected in her concert tour, where she makes sure to put on a good show and always has several costume changes!

Mostly Cs—You have the heart and soul of a musician or an artist. You live for the music, just like Taylor does. For her, it's all about the melodies and lyrics and the way they flow together, expressing more than either could alone.

Mostly Ds—Deep down, Taylor is just an

ordinary teenage girl—just like you! She loves spending time with friends, doing silly things together, and just talking and having fun.

☆☆ CHAPTER 21 ☆☆
Taylor Online

Taylor Swift is always on the move. So, if you want to keep up with country's golden girl, here is a list of websites with all of the latest Taylor information all the time! Taylor would always want you to be careful online. As an advocate for "Delete Online Predators," she would caution you to never give out any sort of personal information—like your name, address, phone number, or the name of your school or sports team—and to never try to meet someone in person that you met online. When you are surfing the Net, you have to remember that not everything you read there is true. So take online information with a grain of salt. And remember, never surf the Web without your parents' permission. Can't find your favorite website? Websites come and go, so don't worry—there's sure to be another Taylor site to replace it soon!

www.taylorswift.com

This is Taylor's official site. It has updates on her projects, tours, videos, photographs, and an online shop where you can buy official Taylor gear.

www.myspace.com/TaylorSwift

This is Taylor Swift's official MySpace page. She checks her page every day and tries to respond to as many fans as possible. So check it out (with your parents' permission, of course) and leave some love for Taylor!

www.taylorswiftlove.com

This is a totally rockin' Taylor fan site. It has pictures, links, video, lots of news updates, and forums where you can chat about all things Taylor.

twitter.com/taylorswift13

Taylor's on Twitter! Subscribe to her Twitter and you can keep up as she posts short comments about touring and recording, details about her day, and messages back and forth with fans and friends!